Achieving Excellence
in Stakeholder Management

Springer
Berlin
Heidelberg
New York
Hong Kong
London
Milan
Paris
Tokyo

Joachim Scharioth · Margit Huber
(Editors)

Achieving Excellence
in Stakeholder Management

With 44 Figures

 Springer

Dr. Joachim Scharioth
Dr. Margit Huber
NFO Infratest
Landsberger Straße 338
80687 München
Germany
joachim.scharioth@nfoeurope.com
margit.huber@nfoeurope.com

ISBN 3-540-00255-3 Springer-Verlag Berlin Heidelberg New York

Cataloging-in-Publication Data applied for
A catalog record for this book is available from the Library of Congress.
Bibliographic information published by Die Deutsche Bibliothek
Die Deutsche Bibliothek lists this publication in the Deutsche Nationalbibliografie; detailed
bibliographic data is available in the Internet at <http://dnb.ddb.de>.

Springer-Verlag Berlin Heidelberg New York
a member of BertelsmannSpringer Science+Business Media GmbH

http://www.springer.de

© Springer-Verlag Berlin · Heidelberg 2003
Printed in Germany

Hardcover-Design: Erich Kirchner, Heidelberg

SPIN 10904930   43/3130/DK – 5 4 3 2 1 0 – Printed on acid-free paper

Preface

Since the 1980s, many businesses have made the question of the customer's needs their central topic of concern. However, customer satisfaction does not automatically imply customer loyalty, which is of central importance to profitability. Today it is generally known that satisfied customers are far from necessarily being loyal customers. A quarter of all customers worldwide are highly satisfied with their suppliers, but with every purchase the decision about which supplier to use is taken anew, due to the fact that many products and services are perceived as similar to others.

This is where the use of an effective Stakeholder Management System is of great advantage.

Stakeholder Management is a term commonly used to describe all interest groups having a stake in a company or an institution (i.e. customers, employees, shareholders). The crucial question is, how it can be best applied to a company's context.

In this book companies using a Stakeholder Management tool give their first-hand account of how this tool enables them to successfully measure, monitor and manage their Stakeholders.

The experience of these companies with Stakeholder Management tools highlights, how across different sectors and countries strong customer relationships, committed employees and successful relationships with suppliers can be created to stay at the forefront of today's global economy.

Munich, November 2002
Dr. Joachim Scharioth, Dr. Margit Huber

Contents

VIII

Introduction
From Customer Satisfaction via Stakeholder Management to the Balanced Scorecard

Dr. Margit Huber, Dr. Joachim Scharioth

Customer Satisfaction as the Starting Point

Since the 1980s, many businesses - starting with companies in the USA - have made the question of the customer's needs a central topic of concern. Based on the principles of Quality Management and the fact that the customer has a view to express, customer satisfaction is continuously being re-examined.
Investigations in this area have enabled businesses to monitor overall satisfaction, but - at least to start with - they offered little indication of the satisfaction levels or otherwise of customers.

At this time, surveys of customer satisfaction were geared strongly towards the idea of quality management. At least since Denning it has been known that additional investment in the product development phase and in production offers significant savings potential and therefore leads to increases in profitability.

This realization was transferred to customer satisfaction in such a manner that every increase of customer satisfaction should itself lead to an enhancement of profitability.

From Customer Satisfaction to Customer Loyalty

But the fact that several businesses highly praised for their outstanding work in the field of customer satisfaction soon afterwards found themselves in serious difficulty showed that customer satisfaction does not automatically imply customer loyalty, which is of central importance to profitability. Today it is generally known that satisfied customers are far from necessarily being loyal customers. A quarter of all customers worldwide are highly satisfied with their suppliers, but with every purchase the decision about which supplier to use is taken anew, due to the fact that many products and services are seen as being very similar to others.

Moreover, it also became clear that measures to increase customer loyalty generally cost more money and that - in contrast to the technical fields - there was a need to estimate very precisely whether investments in greater customer satisfaction are made worthwhile by additional income resulting from greater customer loyalty.
The consequence of this was that interest was now focused more intensely on customer loyalty and efforts were made to discover what factors were primarily responsible for creating customer loyalty. A whole series of model-supported measuring systems were invented to answer the question of what customers perceive as being good or bad, and why they show loyalty - or indeed lack loyalty - to a business.

Customer Loyalty and New Customer Acquisition

Concentrating on customer loyalty alone does not do justice to the full realities of business or market competition, whilst creating customer loyalty without attracting new customers is also a doomed strategy.
Interestingly enough, it was a fairly long time before these two vital factors in customer orientation were no longer regarded as contradictory and for the realization to dawn that satisfied and loyal customers were the best precondition for efficient new customer acquisition. Word-of-mouth recommendation is recognized as a link between these two aims.
Diller brought these ideas together in a three-stage model in 1995. This model recommends firstly building up as intensive and long-lasting a relationship as possible with existing customers, secondly

winning over new customers primarily through personal recommendation from existing customers, and thirdly constantly working on increasing the profitability of every individual customer relationship. Today there is a whole range of measuring systems that aim to answer these questions, although only a few of them take account of the division of roles between measuring and managing.

Models exist that attempt to identify actions to be taken directly from the measurements without considering the fact that the measuring process can only be the basis for management decisions about the areas in which investment should or should not be made.

From Customer Loyalty to Stakeholder Management

At about the same time it was realized that although customer relationships have a high value, if the interests of employees were not also considered, there was a risk of making poor investments. Measures to create customer loyalty borne on the backs of staff members without taking their concerns into account can have precisely the opposite effect as dissatisfied employees frighten customers off rather than attracting them.

The idea that there are other stakeholder groups in a business besides the customers has led to a broadening of viewpoints. Satisfied customers plus satisfied employees does not necessarily equal satisfied stakeholders, because companies that pursue the first two goals often earn very unsatisfactory profits. And while Shareholder Value fails to recognize the principles of Stakeholder Management, concentrating as it does solely on short-term profit, the idea of Shareholder Confidence encompasses a wider view. In the context of Stakeholder Management, for a business this means that its relationship with its shareholders must be measured and managed just as much as, say, customer retention and employee commitment levels.

A business that pays careful attention to external customer loyalty will necessarily come to the realization that internal customer satisfaction also plays a central role, and this leads it into the measurement of internal service quality. The functions farmed out in the context of outsourcing are recorded through measurements relating to the Supplier Partnership.

When measuring Employee Commitment, the enormous significance of leadership often becomes apparent, and this in turn leads to an expansion of the assessment of stakeholder groups to include a Management Evaluation, a field where currently the interplay between psychological manager evaluation systems and empirical management assessment still needs to be optimized.

In the last few years of the 20th century, the concept of the Learning Organization grew in significance. This entails the realization that individual learning and Organizational Learning are far from being inextricably linked. For instance, there are businesses that spend enormous sums on training their staff without being able to use the additional knowledge in their own organization.

Today it is apparent that organizational learning can best be measured by observing the changes in the relationships that a company has with its stakeholder groups. Companies that succeed in achieving sustainable development of "hidden opportunities" to surprise existing and new customers again and again with their efficiency; companies that can turn weaknesses in customer loyalty into strengths are just as vital as companies that continuously enhance the motivation and commitment of their employees. It goes without saying that this applies just as much to the commitment of suppliers as to the confidence of stakeholders. By measuring these changes it is possible to assess the level of Organizational Learning, which we call Vitality.

Stakeholder Management and the Balanced Scorecard

Quite separately from the development of Stakeholder Management, Kaplan and Norton[1] developed their idea of the Balanced Scorecard at the beginning of the 1990s. In it, two thoughts stand in the foreground:
Firstly, a business must not restrict itself purely to pursuing financial indices, not least because this would result in a purely backward view of business strategy. For that reason, Kaplan and Norton widened the horizon by observing customer relations, internal processes and by looking at employee learning and organizational learning.

The second aspect is the integration of a business's strategic orientation - Controlling, i.e. the acquisition of key figures and targets - and operational activity.

These ideas need time to become established and they are only effective when the role distribution within a business is introduced into this framework. In its consideration of strategy and aims, top management must therefore include the effects on the four areas of finance, customers, internal processes, staff and innovation from the very beginning. The Controlling department can then develop the key figures and targets in cooperation with the management based on these strategic principles. It then falls to the operational management to develop methods and actions to meet the targets and thereby to help convert the strategy into reality. Only recently has this role distribution been recognized and defined, although it has increased the realization prospects of the Balanced Scorecard. For as long as a strategic development unit is given the possibility of developing the entire Balance Scorecard from strategy to concrete actions with or without involvement of the actual role players themselves, then the concept is doomed to fail.

---

[1] Robert S. Kaplan, David P. Norton, The Balanced Scorecard: Translating Strategy into Action, Harvard Business School Press, Boston, MA 02163

A second development is slowing down the introduction of the Balanced Scorecard into businesses: committed managers in middle ranking positions use the Balanced Scorecard for their departments with the result that - particularly in large companies - a patchwork of Balanced Scorecards that cannot be compared with each other is produced. Each of them has high local relevance, but is ultimately unusable for the overall business.

In all, there are five requirements for a Balanced Scorecard:

- A forward view rather than a backward view.
- Balance in all four areas.
- Focusing on the most important measures.
- Consistency throughout the entire organization.
- Measurability of all key figures.

Only very gradually is this significance being recognized and implemented in business practice. To date, it is usually only in customer relations and employee commitment that a link exists between the idea of Stakeholder Management and the Balanced Scorecard. However, if one wishes to create a consistent system for an entire company, it becomes apparent that stakeholder relations must be given a high level of importance if comparability between different organizational units is aspired to. In this process, measuring stakeholder relationships becomes the second most important variable for the Balanced Scorecard. Stakeholder Management can therefore become an important link towards making today's department-specific Scorecards comparable again at a higher level of aggregation. When introducing the Balanced Scorecard, stakeholder indices may play a decisive role in strengthening strategic orientation. The interlocking process proposed here therefore reaches its highest point with the idea that financial indices and stakeholder indices are the key strategic indicators of the Balanced Scorecard. They are measured equally for all sectors, while process times and 6 Sigma measurements can be used to represent the sector-specific key figures of the Balanced Scorecard.

If the stakeholder relationship is analyzed in the light of the Balanced Scorecard with a view to consistency in all departments, the following key figures emerge:

- External customer loyalty, measured not only at the whole company level, but as the contribution of every individual business unit to the success of external customer loyalty.

- Internal service quality, which makes clear how strongly each department supports the processes within the company or the extent to which a department inhibits this.

- Employee commitment as the basis for the two key figures addressed above.

- Possibly Management Assessment and, above all, Vitality, which indicates the extent to which a department plays a shaping role in the future development of a company or the extent to which only the past is taken into account.

1 From Customer Satisfaction to Customer Loyalty: The experience of the Michelin and NFO Infratest Workshop

Massimo Leonardi

> *"The real bosses of the economic system are the consumers. If the consumers decide to no longer give their support to a certain business area, the entrepreneurs in that field will be forced to give up the pre-eminent position they occupied in the economic system or align their corporate policy with consumers' desires and needs".*

> **Ludwig von Mises**
> *(Economic policy. Reflections for the present and the future. 1959)*

1.1 Introduction

Anyone who works in the Italian market of car-related products and services cannot fail to have noticed that, alongside the evolution in the forms of competition, deep changes have been taking place for some years in the marketing and selling strategies of the more dynamic operators. In the car tire replacement market, in particular, some of the traditional ways of selling tires and providing the related services have also progressively been changing.

The Italian car tire replacement market is not a small market; some of the world's largest tire manufacturers have production units in this country and many others, of international dimensions, are likewise interested in its volumes, generated by a road population of about 31 million vehicles with one of the highest densities per square kilometer in the world.

As far as distribution is concerned, Italy represents an anomaly compared to the rest of Europe: distribution is on the one hand highly fragmented (the retail trade is characterized by an enormous number of sales-points) and on the other hand, retail sales are concentrated in the channel of the specialist retailers, who sell more than 80% of the replacement car tires purchased by end customers. This situation came about in the years immediately following the last war and its continued existence is also due to the importance that Italian consumers have always attached to their personal relationship with the Specialist Retailer and to the convenience of buying within their close neighborhood.

New distributors, who have made their appearance on the European markets in the last few decades, have struggled to establish themselves in Italy; only recently we are starting to detect the first signs of a change in this situation. Alongside the traditional channel of the Specialist Retailer, we are in fact seeing the development of new commercial concepts such as "car centers", but companies that already operate in this market, such as car traders and authorized dealers, are also including car tires in their product offering.

In addition to the competition between companies operating in the same channel, now there is as well competition between distribution channels based on differing structures and differing approaches to the motorist. They all however have one common objective, namely: to multiply the number of occasions for people to visit the sales-points in order to increase both the customer's *spending* there and their *store loyalty*.

Parallel to this increased competition, customers, too, have changed significantly and not only because of generation changes. The motorist category has become highly fragmented; motorists' needs and expectations are nowadays evolving and diversifying more quickly than in the past. In addition, they find themselves in the position of being able to choose from a more extensive offering of products and services in different sales-points. Therefore it is no longer sufficient to acquire new customers; it is necessary to inspire their loyalty, by establishing a more personalized relationship with them.

This explains the increased attention that distributors are dedicating to customer behavior. Developing and consolidating the relations with customers, through implementation of *customer retention* and *store loyalty* strategies, has become a priority axis for distributors in defining their commercial policies.

In this market context, Michelin invited interested Specialist Retailers to take part in a program based on a common commitment to strive for continuous improvement in the quality of the services supplied to motorists, with the aim of increasing their satisfaction. The constant commitment of the Specialist Retailers would be to increasingly improve the quality of the customer service dispensed in his sales-points; Michelin's constant commitment would be to produce tires that comply more and more with customer needs. Participation in the program involved a yearly qualitative analysis of the sales-points which considered all service-related aspects, evaluated from the customer's viewpoint. The findings of each analysis are certainly not exhaustive. The parameters of the analysis are structural in nature; they certainly constitute a good basis for starting to think about what actions should be initiated, with a view to continually improving the service supplied to motorists; however, they do not take into consideration the particular expectations of the customers of each Specialist Retailer.

In order to obtain information concerning what customers are expecting and how satisfied they are with the services provided at the individual sales-points, it was decided to make available a specific survey to the Specialist Retailers taking part in the program. This survey was not simply and solely a measuring tool, but also and above all a proactive instrument, that would help define courses of action to raise customer satisfaction levels and increase *customer retention*. Michelin was looking for the most suitable method for fulfilling this need; the Specialist Retailer, if interested in exploring the expectations of his customers and in measuring their degree of satisfaction with the services they received, would be able to commission the chosen Company to conduct the survey at his sales-point.

In these last few years the Companies have invested and continue to invest in research on the satisfaction of end customers, with a large number of research techniques being available. Michelin evaluated the various different possibilities in order to identify a method that the Specialist Retailers would regard as suitable for measuring the satisfaction of the customers in their sales-points.

NFO Infratest's approach to the problem (the TRI*M method together with its tools: the TRI*M Index, the Grid and the Actiogram) certainly fulfilled this objective. What was even more satisfactory however was NFO Infratest's consultation in defining the research objectives and the ways in which these should be presented to the people taking part in the program.

1.2   The Michelin and NFO Infratest workshop

In structuring the research process, the first step was to get the Michelin sales force *management* to agree on the research objectives and fieldwork technique. The fruitful and interactive discussion with the NFO Infratest researchers on how to manage the customer satisfaction was fundamental.

The *briefings* provided understanding of the "circular process of customer satisfaction" and of the concept that attention and orientation to customer satisfaction is the "business" of every single person employed at the sales-point and not just of those who are in direct contact with motorists.

The meetings ensured that the research approach proposed by NFO Infratest was understood and internalized, namely: to carry out qualitative research in order, on one hand, to determine the dynamics that are set in motion and then govern the Italian motorist's choice of sales-point and tire and, on the other hand, to identify all the factors that play a significant role in determining the customer satisfaction and his/her perception of quality. The findings of the qualitative stage were used to draw up a questionnaire based on the convictions and the behaviors of the motorist who uses the sales point of a particular Specialist Retailer.

However, the aspect relating to the presentation of the survey and of the TRI*M method to the Specialist Retailers interested still remained open.

Over the years, operators in the car tire replacement market have developed a strong sell-in culture, paying less attention to the sell-out, with the result that the Specialist Retailers have developed price-focused commercial policies. Generally speaking, little use was made of the other variables in the marketing-mix to promote processes of customer loyalty.

Presenting a research without giving practical examples of how the results could be used in order to define what improvements, if any, could be made and what priority should be given to them, appeared to be somewhat difficult, and this in spite of the perceived needs for change and consequent greater sensitivity and propensity to develop an equally strong sell-out culture, oriented to offering new and differentiated services to suit customers' differing expectations. It was therefore decided to conduct the survey at both national and local levels, taking in the first case a representative sample of recent buyers of car tires at sales-points belonging to Specialist Retailers covering the whole of Italy and, in the second case, conducting the research in a specific sales-point of a Specialist Retailer taking part in the program who, of course, remained anonymous. The findings of these two surveys were presented during the course of a specific meeting arranged and led jointly by Michelin and NFO Infratest.

Those taking part in the meeting were able to find out what Italian motorists are satisfied with and why, what they are not satisfied with and why. In addition, they had the opportunity of evaluating the contribution made by the TRI*M method in pinpointing where action should be taken and its support in defining the best type of ameliorative action to carry out, according to priorities based on the needs and expectations expressed by the customers themselves.

At the same time, it was realized that the average evaluation for Italy was different to that expressed for the individual sales-point and in the final analysis, that it could differ from what their customers might have expressed if the research had been conducted in their sales-points. As a result, since each Specialist Retailer had locally different types of customer, carrying out the study amongst their own customers would have made it possible to target the improvement activities with no waste of effort, resources and energy. In order to help determine how action plans could be defined by analyzing the findings of the research and to appreciate the TRI*M method's function as support to the decisions, the participants were divided into a number of work groups in order to identify the possible actions that could be implemented at the sales-point for the purpose of improving the judgment expressed by the customers in the national survey. The work group was instructed to regard itself as the owner of the sales-point who was examining the survey findings and, more in particular, the items that had proved to be negative. Using the support of the TRI*M Grids, the possible alternative courses of action were formulated for the purpose of improving the customers' evaluation with regard to each individual factor which had shown the need for priority action.

In this way, the objective of "training" the Specialist Retailers to make effective use of the research findings was achieved.

In addition, a document containing the work of each group was handed over to all people taking part in the meeting. Accordingly, for each item considered by the research, possible guidelines, indications and incentives were provided for improving the customers evaluation and, as a result, increasing their store loyalty, perhaps satisfying "an old need in a new way".

1.3 Conclusions

Since it is not possible to report the experiences of every Specialist Retailer who carried out the survey, we shall accordingly limit ourselves to making some general considerations with regard to the "added value" offered by the TRI*M method in defining the *customer retention* strategies.

It certainly made a sizeable contribution to increase the Specialist Retailer's awareness that customers can choose whether to buy the products and services that they want from him or from someone else. As a result a smile or a special "friendly" price is no longer sufficient to satisfy the customer and obtain his loyalty. The research findings have made the Specialist Retailer aware of the need to improve his level of attention to the behavior of his customers and helped him realize that his customers, too, have changed and will continue to change.

Some of the Retailers who carried out the survey realized for the first time that their customers look at what surrounds them and notice immediately what does not work the way it should. Their satisfaction or dissatisfaction is determined by the work of the whole organization and not only by the price they pay for the product they buy.

As a result, the research findings were used not only to improve the quality of the services provided at the sales-point, but also to improve the quality of the interrelations between company employees and customers. Presenting the findings to the employees made it possible, on the one hand, to get the whole organization to realize that managing the relations with customers implies and requires knowledge and awareness of both the customers' expectations and their degree of satisfaction with the services they have received, defining and implementing improvements, the desire to monitor changes in the customers' expectations and satisfaction and, on the other hand, to get the employees to assimilate the fact, if they want to guarantee the future, they have to think, believe and want customers to be able to obtain from the company a service, a value that they cannot find elsewhere.

In a competitive context, in which every player in the market is under pressure, it is certainly not easy to be self-critical and be able to continuously question one's role and performance, but it is equally true that *customer retention* is directly related to the entire company's ability and to its degree of customer orientation and, as a result, the satisfaction of the customer is the priority "business" of all those who form part of it.

This, briefly, is the "message" that in general came out of the analysis of the findings of the research carried out by a number of Specialist Retailers using the TRI*M method proposed by NFO Infratest.

2 What makes TRI*M Methodology effective in improving quality?

Luigi Ciuti

2.1 Procter and Gamble is a quality-oriented company

Procter and Gamble (P&G) is a USA based Company operating in the FMCG and in the pharmaceutical markets. It has branches in 140 countries and turnover is higher than 40 billion dollars.

P&G is universally known for the importance it dedicates to research and quality. The mission of our company is "To supply quality products of superior value which improve the everyday life of consumers". To support this aim, we have a Research and Development Department with over 7.000 researchers with an average of 3.800 patents per year.

The same quality is applied to our Customers' Service. We recognize that we must have a win-win approach and be ready to grow with them. Our Sales Department changed the name into Customer Business Development to signify our attention to them.

In Italy, P&G is present since 1956 with commercial, technical centers and plants.

2.2   To be always up to the intended quality we track it regularly

In the Consumer & Market Knowledge (CMK) Department, among many other tasks, we help our colleagues in R&D, Marketing and CBD to fulfill at best our quality promise with consumers and customers.

To guide our benchmarking work, we set up a series of research aimed at comparing our performance against both Consumers' expectations and our Competitor's performance. This kind of research is standard and regularly conducted in all our key markets through a system of research that we designed internally.

The standardization is quite important for a Global Company like ours, where we need to compare data coming from all over the world. On the other side, we are always open to research market to find and try innovative technologies that can enhance our understanding of consumers and customers.

2.3   TRI*M is a promising technique to track the quality that we provide

Through the above idea of introducing innovative research techniques, in Italy we recently tested a research method, called TRI*M by NFO Infratest.

I cannot expand, for confidentiality reasons, on the specific research that we conducted, so I will illustrate a classical use.

TRI*M is a classical Consumer/ Customer Satisfaction Study, it asks rating on several aspects of the Brand/ Company's performance: starting from Overall and Convenience Ratings and then going into details through specific performance statements.

The key measures you can get from TRI*M are:

- TRI*M Index: This is a standard indicator based on the Overall and the Convenience rating. These two values are averaged, with different weights, to obtain the Index.

- TRI*M Grid: This is a map that visually shows the risks and opportunities for all the Companies included in the study.

- TRI*M Actiogram: This is the specific action plan that can be derived from the above findings.

These measures are providing in my view, at least two added values versus usual Satisfaction Studies:

- The cross Market standardization. Since the TRI*M index is standard, NFO Infratest can compare results not only against the competitors that we have chosen, but can also provide indication of best in class in other markets.

- The sophisticated statistical treatment of results that are used to create the Grid. The resulting maps are very powerful in summarizing results so that is very easy to agree on how the Actiogram should look like.

The latter advantage is the one on which I want to concentrate in this paper, as the former is self-explanatory.

2.4   Usual satisfaction studies

For market researchers, it is a very common problem to understand how much the answers they are getting are driven by "claimed" or by "real" influence.

For example, the following table could show ratings on several items for some Companies being tested:

Table 1

The Company provides	Company			
	A	B	C	D
Cooperation with trade	70	65	65	72
Info on consumers	10	25	13	12
Product innovation	15	25	35	15
Clear commercial conditions	80	75	83	79

This would give us the Equity of each company in the study. However, we still do not know which is the importance of each item. So, we can add an Importance rating question for each of those items. These are the results:

Table 2

It is important that the Company ensures:	
Cooperation with Trade	80
Info on Consumers	35
Product Innovation	40
Clear Commercial Conditions	95

The usual way of analyzing these tables is through Gap analysis, i.e. by subtracting from the Importance rating the rating each Company is scoring on that item.

Table 3

The Company provides	Company			
	A	B	C	D
Cooperation with trade	-10	-15	-15	-8
Info on consumers	-25	-10	-22	-23
Product innovation	-25	-15	-5	-15
Clear Commercial Conditions	-15	-20	-12	-16

So we can conclude that all companies, while strong in the first and last items, should still improve their performance on these items as they are the most important ones and still have a gap to fill. Also Company C looks ahead compared to the others.

But is this true?

I doubt it is true and would be very worried to make recommendations based on that chart because it is too influenced by "claimed" data!

Some items, usually the most important ones are a "must" or with another definition "a cost of entry". No Company would be able to sell a detergent that is NOT cleaning the laundry, nor Trade would consider a Company with unclear Commercial Conditions. But is it really wise to invest even more effort to improve performance when it is already obviously high? Or would it not be smarter to work on other characteristics that may not be so highly rated but are indeed important?

The issue is how to find out which are the "real" important items, and more specifically, how we can separate "claimed" from "real" influence.

For example, a way of taking out the cost of entry is Normalization. If we normalize the table by taking out from the respondents' answers the average row effect, a procedure well documented in different papers, we can already see a different picture.

Table 4

The Company provides	Company			
	A	B	C	D
Cooperation with Trade	2	-3	-3	4
Info on consumers	-5	10	-2	-3
Product Innovation	-8	3	13	-8
Clear Commercial Conditions	1	-4	4	0

If we look at Company C, we can see that its highest score, on Clear Commercial Conditions, is very high in absolute (83), still far from ideal (95), but ahead of market average (+4). What should we conclude with so many different numbers? Should I spend money and resources to improve in this area, or not? Also, compared to other Companies, it looks strong mainly on item #3, but is it the correct one to hit the market?

2.5 TRI*M Grid as corner stone of efficient performance improvement

To find real importance of each item, TRI*M makes a multidimensional analysis to explain the TRI*M index results by using the performance items. By doing this we create a statistical method where the importance is measured by the power of each item in explaining the TRI*M Index variance.

However, unlike other approaches that only use the calculated importance instead of claimed ones, TRI*M uses both of them in a holistic way.

This adds a real twist to the research. In fact, we can find the real influence, but we also need to recognize that respondents still truly believe in what they were claiming to be important. We cannot forget their will because we have calculated one that looks better at explaining their behavior.

By creating a map that has as two dimensions, the "claimed" importance and "real" importance, we are ready to understand what our Consumers/ Customers are asking us what they may be ready to accept once we make clearer how important it is to them, even if they have not realized it yet.

Now, we only need to take into account each Company's performance on these items versus competition and we have quite another picture than the one coming from table 3.

Chart no. 1: TRI*M Grid for Company X

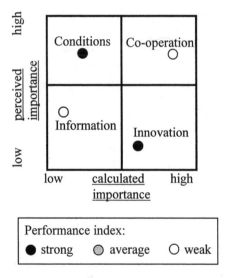

Cooperation is very important on both dimensions (but the Company is not so strong here), but commercial Conditions (where the Company is strong) do not influence so much on the TRI*M Index, they are a cost of entry.

If you have a good performance here it is enough; you do not need to improve further. On the other side, there is a greater opportunity to exploit on Innovation. The influence on the TRI*M Index is very high, but you must help the Trade to understand this. The company that it is best positioned to do so is Company C that, once normalized versus the row averages, has the highest score on this item.

So we can answer the question I asked previously at the end of section 4: yes this is the correct item to hit the market. However, I can now make this statement with much greater confidence because I much better understand the dynamics that work in the market.

2.6 Conclusion

The TRI*M techniques proved to be very good at bringing together several pieces of information in such a cohesive way to make the creation of a specific action plan easier.

Specifically, TRI*M links "claimed" and "real" importance rating in such a way that is preserving the information contained in each of them, while putting the relative strengths of each brand/ company versus the market average into proper perspective.

3 Research on Czech Telecom Customer Retention

Petr Skokan

*We began the measurement of CZECH TELECOM customer reten-
tion in 1996. This step was closely connected with the sale in 1995
of a 25% share of the company to a foreign investor. The newly-in-
coming managers were used to standard customer satisfaction research, and therefore the launch of such a project in CZECH
TELECOM came about very quickly. Customer retention measurement, based on the TRI*M methodology, has continued ever since.*

From the very beginning, the goal of the continuous customer survey
was to give the Quality Department a tool with which to measure
and improve company procedures, as seen from the customer's perspective. At the same time it provides the top management, and
above all the Sales & Marketing Department, with information about
the company's competitive position in the market.

It is helpful to describe the environment in which CZECH
TELECOM operated back in the mid-nineties, and its development
since that time. During the major part of the nineties the Czech telecommunications sector underwent extensive growth. From 1994 to
2000 the number of fixed lines more than doubled, penetration
reached 40 telephones per 100 inhabitants, and the rate of
digitization rose from zero to more than 80%. In 1996, while this
development of a fixed network was continuing, the first two GSM
operators started offering their services, and after the introduction of
pre-paid services, mobile telephones rapidly started to compete with
traditional telephones in the area of voice services. By the end of the
year 2000 it is expected that the total number of mobile phones will
exceed the number of fixed lines. At the same time, the 1st of
January 2001 was also the date of full liberalization of the telecom-

munications market in this country. Until then, CZECH TELECOM was able to exclusively offer domestic and international voice services.

In the light of this situation, the original task of the customer retention measurement was to provide information about how the customers see the development of the company in the defined key areas. To identify this, the research focused on the following five areas:

- Basic telephone services;
- Installation of new lines;
- Fault repairs;
- Billing claims;
- Operator services.

Later on, specialized projects focusing on top customers were added to these areas, and since 1999 the focus has also shifted towards the sales performance of the company. This led to the special 6th research area, evaluating the Sales activities from the customer's point of view. Since 1997, continuous research and monitoring of employee loyalty and satisfaction, based on TRI*M methodology, has also been conducted. To complete the set, research focused on the overall company image is also regularly carried out (twice a year), which puts the specialized customer satisfaction research into a wider context, and the results to be placed within a more general environment.

The results of both the customer and employee retention research serve to set planning criteria for the business and annual plans of the company and its individual units. In the performance evaluation methodology (the balanced score cards) used in CZECH TELECOM since 1998, two of the most essential criteria are customer and employee retention, measured by the TRI*M Index. This means that the overall remuneration of all managers in the company depends directly on the results achieved in the areas of customer and employee satisfaction *(see Chart no. 1)*.

To follow on from the evolution of customer retention research, we have developed a system of reporting that uses two types of report – monthly signal reports and quarterly analyses. The monthly reports focus on immediate developments in the customer's point of view, according to the following indicators:

- TRI*M Index development;
- Customer portfolio;
- Development of satisfaction in the most important areas.

The monitoring of the TRI*M Index is especially aimed at senior management level, and serves as a tool which gives a brief overview of the development of defined areas and segments of the market. This result is then accompanied by the Customer portfolio description, which provides important information on the competitiveness of the company in individual market segments. For the line managers, the development of individual items within their fields of responsibility is particularly important. These are either represented by the TRI*M Grid, or by tracking the development of satisfaction with individual items. These monthly reports are prepared internally in the Sales Support Department.

Chart no. 1: Planning and evaluation cycle

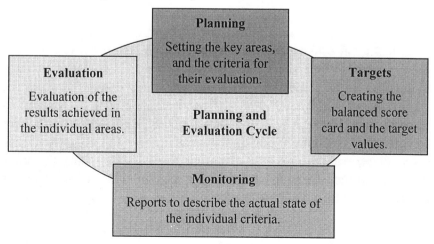

The quarterly analysis is more detailed and is prepared by AISA. These reports aim to describe the latest trends in customers' opinions, and describe the existing threats and opportunities. The basic tool for these reports is the TRI*M Grid analysis and TRI*M Grid development.

It is of fundamental importance that the research corresponds with the current progress of company processes, and to this end there are several teams, each of which supervise a certain stage of the individual process. As a result, it is especially possible to work on changes in the services offered (this refers mostly to adjustments of the questionnaires) and to react to the implementation of new systems (data collection). Based in particular on the longer-term threats, these teams also serve as "generators" of ideas about how to solve problem areas, and in defined cases they can also propose solutions and prepare projects which are then implemented across the company by line management.

To name some of the latest activities, or to give an idea of the problems tackled by the teams, the work has lately focused on simplifying the administration of customer contact (implementation of new types of document and methods of placing orders – especially using the Internet). Attention is also being paid to improvements in the quality of certain procedures, such as faster installation and connected services, and the minimization of the number of repeated faults in the area of Fault Repair.

As we have seen a shift in customer focus during the last few years from technical criteria (network quality, connection clarity, etc) towards more customer-orientated services, customer research also has to develop in the same way. The customers now demand a faster response, more highly qualified staff, and easier means of contact. In order to keep in touch with this development, large-scale qualitative research was carried out during this year, to give the necessary feedback for re-evaluation of the customer research focus and to facilitate the correct reaction to changing customer expectations *(see Chart no. 2)*.

Chart no. 2: Customer Retention Research Development

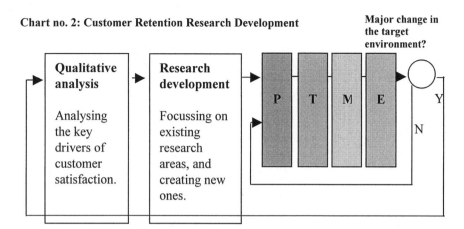

This is a key role of the customer retention research – we must provide the senior and line management with information that is always relevant to the individual types of service and customer in the respective market segments. This will deliver enough data for the implementation of decisions which are correct from the customer's perspective.

4 Haspa Quality – from Customer Satisfaction to Customer Retention

Andreas Capell

4.1 Development of a fully integrated quality management procedure

Throughout the 1990's, the importance of quality management has increased for organizations and has by now become one of the cornerstones of company policies. Nowadays, customers have specific expectations with regard to the quality of the service they receive. Especially in relation to the competition, this makes on-going improvements necessary.

Having been mainly limited to the manufacturing industries earlier on, the change of focus towards quality as well has increasingly encompassed the service industries in recent years. Many times customers have experienced the cliché of non-existent service and customer care themselves. As banks are offering virtually identical product portfolios, the decisive factor for choosing a bank, or for the success of an existing customer relationship, is more often than not the provision of customer- and quality-orientated services.

What follows is a detailed report of Hamburger Sparkasse's experiences with developing and continuously running a fully integrated quality management procedure.

4.1.1 History of a quality concept

The reason for Hamburger Sparkasse – in short Haspa - to embark on specific activities to facilitate quality assurance in 1993, was a perceived increase in customer dissatisfaction with Haspa's services.

Furthermore, activities of competitors, e.g. the market entry of direct banks, led to an increase in competition that Haspa, in their traditional position as Hamburg's no. 1 financial institution, had to face. The customers' continuously changing and rising expectations also played a strong role in the decision to develop a comprehensive quality concept, and then make this concept a living part of the company culture in order to be prepared for the exceedingly difficult future challenges of the banking sector.

During the course of this process, the unanimous emphasis was placed on not creating a project that would run for a limited period of time, but on designing a process that would continuously adapt to the needs of the marketplace. This process exclusively relies on the Haspa employees, as they are the ones who come face to face with the customers and have to live up to the customers' expectations.

4.1.2 Bottom up – "Experience it for yourself and be empowered to act"

The fact that the relationship between employees and customers has been, and still is, the pillar on which activities to facilitate an increase in quality are based, made it easy to decide on the method that would be employed to implement quality management. The decision was made not to introduce Haspa to the aspect of quality by means of the commonly used concept-orientated "top down"-approach, but to opt for a more practical approach that could become an integral part of the individual employees' service and performance experience and this within a reasonably short period of time after the implementation.

At the same time, the conceptual element was not to be neglected in order to assure that the foundations of the quality management procedure were preserved. Due to these reasons, two parallel paths have been taken since 1993; both of them have been continuously adapted to new developments and requirements:

Approaches for a fully integrated practical quality management procedure:

Chart no. 1

> Concept-orientated Approach:
>
> Gathering all elements that are conceptually relevant for establishing fully integrated quality management

> Practical Approach: "Bottom up"
>
> Actively incorporating all employees working in the branches and service centres, as well as those in administrative positions in the quality management procedure

According to the motto 'Haspa Quality – Count Me In!' Quality Teams have been created as a tool to put further emphasis on the active integration of employees into the quality management procedure ("bottom up"). Quality Teams are committees consisting of employees in branches, service centers and administrative departments. In team meetings that are chaired by a discussion leader, they look to develop measures that will increase the satisfaction of the respective customer target groups: private customers for branches, individual customers (= wealthy private customers) for special service centers, and corporate customers.

The focus of the teams' activities is not on putting the blame for as many mistakes as possible on those other persons who prevent oneself from delivering high quality. On the contrary, in their analyses they almost exclusively concentrate on their own attitude towards their customers and on showing more customer orientation when organizing their workload.

The meaning of 'customer' in this context is not limited to the customers who are using Haspa's services at the cashier, at the service desk or when consulting their personal banker (external customers). It also includes the employees themselves (internal customers) when they require information, assistance or co-operation from their colleagues within the company.

In order to get all the employees into the right mood for teamwork, external trainer held one-day 'kick-off' events. Almost every single Haspa employee participated in one of those events between 1993 and 1998. The main emphasis of these events was on personal contact with the customers, co-operating as a customer-orientated team, and each employee's personal attitude when dealing with their customers and their expectations – both with regard to the respective employee and with regard to Haspa.

The Quality Teams were (and are) free to choose the topics of their teamwork. However, one of the main issues was to focus on the customers' expectations from a theoretical as well as practical point of view. In the past, the choice of topics very clearly showed that dealing with (service) quality on a very frequent level, results also in dealing with basic interactions on a daily basis:

Chart no. 2: Set topics for the quality teams

Interaction with colleagues and customers
Reducing Waiting Times
Telephone Manners
Optimising Procedures
Cross-departmental co-operation
Handling of customers' complaints

During the past few years, especially the Quality Teams in branches and service centers, developed an increasing tendency to choose their topics in relation to recent changes within the organization, e.g. the implementation of new sales structures and the effects this has on the individual employee. Nonetheless, being prepared to deliver customer-orientated services – "service mentality" - is a recurrent topic that forms a regular part of the daily agenda. The idea behind it is that, in the long run, a lack of the 'right' attitude towards the customer prevents a successful customer relationship, and customer retention.

4.1.3 Correlation of single quality management

Since 1993, Haspa's quality management procedure has continuously undergone further development and adaptations to latest requirements. By now, four cornerstones of the quality management procedure have been linked through their various interfaces:

Chart no. 3: Components of quality management / market research

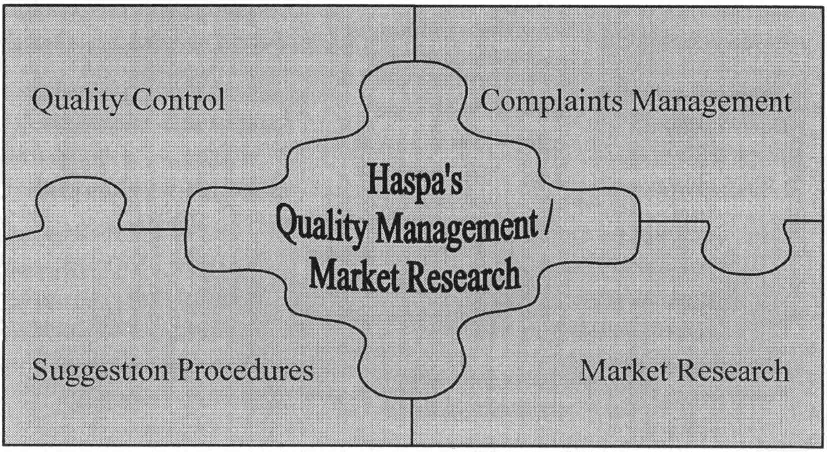

The **Quality Control** component is the Quality Team approach taken to the next level. It mainly focuses on a process of continuous improvement that actively involves the employees within each part of the organization, be it a branch, service center or administrative department.

Complaints Management relates to collecting, processing and analyzing complaints from customers and so-called 'opinion leaflets'. Every complaining customer gives the organization a hint relating to a perceived flaw. This procedure enables Haspa to subject their services to continuous process of improvement and to adapt their services to their customers' expectations. Thus, complaints should not be viewed as a nuisance, but as a chance - even more so as it is not unusual, that if a complaint that has been excellently handled may result in a stronger relationship between Haspa and a customer. Excellent complaints management is a useful tool for retaining customers.

Employees' suggestions are being collected and analyzed by means of **Suggestion Procedures**, which are also employed in preparing the decision-making process for the implementation of a suggestion. An organization that puts the customers' needs first requires every single employee, more than ever, to be creative and prepared to perform. Nobody has better knowledge of the working conditions on a day-to-day basis under which services are being delivered, or of the individual needs of the customers, than the employees themselves.

Haspa's internal **Market Research** refers to the systematic collection, processing, analysis and interpretation of market data, in order to gather information that decision-making processes can be based upon. The interfaces of this component become more apparent through the measuring tools that relate to quality.

These four components are not only linked with regard to their contents, but are also represented as an integrated administrative 'Quality Management / Market Research' department. A team of employees' processes the multitude of tasks derived from the respective topics, evaluates those tasks in relation to each other and deducts measures that are to be implemented during the course of the organization's quality management procedure. The ability to measure quality is gaining increasing significance in this context.

4.2 Measuring quality

„You can only improve on what can be measured " – After the quality management procedure had been launched via the Quality Teams, a second phase begun in 1997. In this phase, the measurability of quality is enforced. At the moment this only takes place with regard to the quality of externally directed services; to accomplish that we use several tools:

Chart no. 4: Methods for measuring customer satisfaction

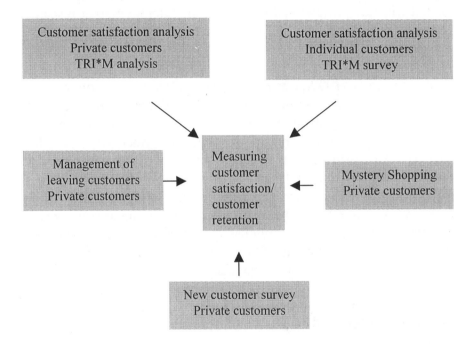

4.2.1 Analyzing Customer Satisfaction and Retention

After a very intense phase of Quality-Team work that hit the highest point at a total of up to 330 teams being active in the front and back office, in 1996 employees and executives increasingly felt the necessity to employ more binding regulations for the quality management procedure. In some cases individual branches, being supported by the Quality Management/Market Research depart-ment, already conducted customer surveys. The branches were able to use the findings of those surveys for creating a provisional profile of their strengths and weaknesses. Although these profiles were of limited significance, they enabled the branches to achieve stronger orientation towards customers' needs.

It was then decided to move away from those rather customized sur-veys of individual branches and service centers towards streamlined customer satisfaction surveys that equally applied to all parts of the organization with customer contact. These surveys were to be con-ducted with the professional support of an external market research company in order to gain definite knowledge relating to customers' expectations.

In the spring of 1997, Haspa decided not only to interview their customers with regard to their satisfaction with the services and per-formance of the organization, but also to collect information relating to customer retention by means of a customer retention index, the TRI*M index. After having gained some experience with the new measurement tool during the same year, annual analyses of customer satisfaction and retention has taken place throughout the whole organization since 1998; these surveys related to the area of private customers. A survey of individual customers was first conducted across the organization in 2000. Again, this survey represents a measuring tool for customer satisfaction and retention. It is also conducted on an on-going basis. It is planned to interview corporate customers with regard to their satisfaction with Haspa's services and the strength of their relationship with Haspa at a later stage.

In 2001, the conducted analyses covered a total of 191 branches and 41 service centers for individual customers. The opinions of a ran-dom sample of approximately 158.000 private customers and approximately 30.000 individual customers have been requested during three waves of the survey. The response rate met the expectations market research experts had, with regard to a survey at this scale that was conducted by means of self-completion question-naires.

The customers received a two-page questionnaire. Apart from questions relating to customer retention, this questionnaire contained a number of quality-related aspects that were to be rated: friendliness, helpfulness, performance with regard to consulting etc. The customers are not asked to give their opinions on the importance of those quality-related aspects (stated importance); the prime reason for this is the overall length of the questionnaire. After the survey has been concluded, this stage is replaced by calculations that result in a statistical positioning of the importance of each quality-related aspect (real importance). For the organisation as a whole, the next step then is to analyze the real importance in relation to the perceived performance of Haspa, with regard to the same quality-related aspects. As a consequence, the so-called Importance-Performance-Portfolio enables to help identify areas that need to be prioritized when it comes to potential improvement within Haspa.

Chart no. 5: Importance - Performance Portfolio

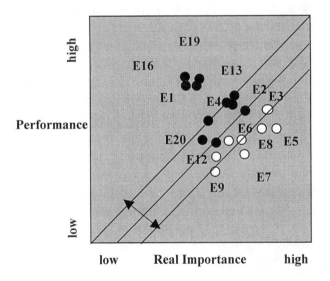

By means of the continuously conducted annual survey for measuring the service-quality and consulting, and also by simultaneously integrating the findings into Haspa's process of setting targets, the idea of quality becomes more binding for all levels in the area of sales. For the branches and service centers for individual customers, the analyses of strengths and weaknesses that have been named by customers, are offering valuable hints that assist in determining factors that are relevant to customer retention. Areas where action has to be taken can be identified, regardless of the question whether such an area only relates to a branch, service center or Haspa as a whole; as a result, operational measures can be initiated. Through the TRI*M index, the intensity of customer retention can be measured at any point. Thus, the index enables internal benchmarking and also helps to identify Haspa's external positioning within the German banking sector.

4.2.2   Mystery Shopping

Haspa perceives the Mystery Shopping, in which branches can participate on a voluntary base, to be a qualitative tool that is complementary to the quantitative customer satisfaction survey of private customers. The Mystery Shopping is also conducted in co-operation with an external market research company.

Mystery Shopping aims at providing a better insight into branch-specific priorities and weaknesses that have been established by the representative annual customer satisfaction survey in order to identify potential sources of respective problems. Furthermore, these tests provide branches with even more detailed impulses for quality-related activities. During Mystery Shopping, reasons for dissatisfaction can be pinpointed through observable circumstances and the subjective impressions of the tester. The employees' actual conduct when engaging in personal contact with customers is the pivotal point of the analysis. The testers' impression of the extent to which the employees' conduct, influenced the successful completion of a sales exercise in a "real-life" consulting also forms a part of this.

Furthermore, the individual case studies are also taking the professional aspects of a consulting into account. The testers are checking whether the respective employee provided the customer with mandatory information and/or consulting services. They pay special attention to the question whether customers' expectations regarding this aspect have not been fulfilled and whether the sales exercise has not been successful for that reason.

In 2001, a total of 290 Mystery Shopping have been conducted in Haspa branches. The testers had the choice of testing 10 different cases that could be employed according to branch-specific priorities and weaknesses.

4.2.3   New customer survey

As early as from 1996, a survey particularly targeting those private customers who opened a current account with Haspa as "genuinely" new customers (young customers with no previous bank account, new customers moving from outside Haspa's area of business, previous customers of other banks) has been conducted. By means of a self-completion questionnaire, these new customers were interviewed about their impressions of the service quality Haspa delivers. Private customers who only switched from one Haspa branch to another are not included in this survey.

This survey is done to increase customer retention as well as to exert quality control with regard to the service experience right at the start of the customer relationship. Moreover, additional market research findings about new customers are to be collected.

According to the motto "Your opinion is important to us", new customers receive a questionnaire by mail approximately 6 to 8 weeks after they have opened their account. This questionnaire includes questions relating to the reasons for choosing Haspa, the quality and extent of first contact and the customers' overall impression. The branches receive an evaluation of the questionnaires that relate to them on an annual basis.

The questions included in the new customer survey and the customer satisfaction survey is synchronized with regard to some specific quality-related aspects; thus, comparisons are possible. The new customer survey also contains questions on how important those quality-related aspects (stated importance) are to the customer. Therefore it is possible to gain some insight into the expectations, that new customers have especially, regarding Haspa, and to gather information on potential gaps between importance and perceived performance at the same time.

4.2.4   Management of leaving customers

The term management of leaving customers describes activities that aim at determining the reasons why customers have left the bank, at analyzing those reasons and at developing counter-measures in order to facilitate a higher level of customer retention.

There are various reasons why customers wish to close their accounts; they range from "moving house" to "better terms and conditions with a new bank" or "being annoyed about an individual employee's conduct". Only a minority of former customers actually gives specific reasons. Furthermore, it happens often enough that the employees themselves are not considering the "real" reasons why customers are leaving. Requirements regarding any documentation of reasons why customers leave, or their communication within Haspa, have not been fulfilled in a consistent manner.

In 2000 leaving customers received a questionnaire with the request to give reasons why they have left Haspa. All the returned questionnaires have been evaluated, the results were used to develop and implement specific preventive measures. It is our aim to put an "early warning system" into practice in order to actively approach customers who are likely to leave and, hence, increase customer retention.

4.3   The executives' role in Quality Management

The executives have always played an important role throughout the whole quality management procedure so far. This role will surely increase in importance in the future, as the dynamics of changes within the organization – changes that of course also effect the quality management procedure – require executives, more than anybody else, to adapt to the present situation and indeed to help shape that situation.

When first embarking on quality management activities, Haspa intended to actively integrate the employees into the improvement process - as part of the bottom-up approach - by the means of the aforementioned Quality Teams.

Increasing the quality of the service was to be facilitated mainly through employees' ideas and suggestions. During this phase of the quality management procedure executives had to take a leading role that enabled the employees to develop their own creative ideas. The employees themselves were to be the main driving force behind the shift towards improvement. At the same time, it frequently became evident that much depended on the executives' commitment towards supporting their employees' ideas and helping with their implementation.

By now, Hamburger Sparkasse has developed a Haspa Leadership Code; the personnel development department played a leading role in this effort. This code explains the common definition of successful leadership to executives and employees of the organization alike.

Chart no. 6: Aspects of leadership: what is expected from executives

Entrepreneurship .... Act like an entrepreneur!
Coaching competence .... Support towards an aim!
Social competence .... Convince through your personality!
Team leading competence .... Develop teams!
Organizational competence .... Work efficiently!
Professional competence .... Learn all your life!

A number of basic principles have been developed to explain the respective levels of leadership and the expectations that are associated with it in greater detail.

To implement the Haspa Leadership Code, the "Competent Leadership" project has been created. This project is not to be viewed as being on the same level with other processes to facilitate change, e.g. quality management. In fact, it rather fuels all other processes and projects.

"Leadership by Objectives" is the foremost tool employed to conceive change within the scope of the "Competent Leadership" project. "Leadership with Objectives" means that executives and employees are discussing the future together: what is the business plan of the company and what are the employees' personal aims? How can those involved reach those aims?

The prerequisite of leadership with objectives are the objectives themselves. The following 5 categories of objectives and targets form the base of Haspa's process of setting targets:

Chart no. 7: Categories of objectives and targets

SUCCESS TARGETS
Which factors should be increased?
QUALITY TARGETS
What will make our customers be even more satisfied?
INNOVATION TARGETS
Which work-related processes have to be improved?
PERSONNEL DEVELOPMENT AND LEADERSHIP OBJECTIVES
How can I lead my employees / my team towards success?
OBJECTIVES FOR PERSONAL DEVELOPMENT
Which areas can I improve in?

The "Quality Targets" of the branches and service centers are agreed upon on the base of the findings of the customer satisfaction and customer retention analyses. Thus, a strong interface has been created between measuring quality and the process of setting targets.

Furthermore, the target categories "Success Targets" and "Quality Targets" will form factors of an upcoming variable benefits system to determine bonuses. This, too, emphasizes Haspa's orientation towards a tighter bond between success and quality.

Chart no. 8: Excerpt from the Haspa Business Guidelines

We want our customers to be satisfied. -
Our attention is focused on the customer.

We want to achieve an even higher level of quality. -
To facilitate future success, we require excellent, reliable quality throughout the whole of Haspa

In future, it will continue to be the executives' task to stress these basic guidelines towards their employees again and again. What is more, they also have to present a model example from their employees' point of view when it comes to adhering to those guidelines during phases of difficult change.

At this point it is worth mentioning the Haspa Quality Charter that defines the required minimum level of quality throughout the organization by the means of setting quality standards. Every employee has received a copy of this printed charter and is required to apply these standards to his or her daily work. It is the executives' responsibility more than anybody else's to coach this process and to also manage the obvious aspects of good practice, e.g. answering the phone in the correct manner, wearing a name tag when having direct customer contact, using the customers' names when greeting them and saying good-bye etc.

Often the incorrect assumption is made that those obvious aspects of good practice have become the employees' second nature by now, and that one should therefore focus on more essential, i.e. current topics of quality management. The customers, however, are frequently proving this notion to be wrong by pointing out that the importance of those taken-for-granted aspects has not decreased in the slightest. It is the executives' responsibility to successfully link the current topics to the taken-for-granted aspects of day-to-day contact with the customers in order to consolidate the aim of "best excellence" in all areas.

4.4 Communications

Communicating activities have been, and continue to be, an essential part of Haspa's quality management procedure. During the course of the past few years, employees have been informed about the current situation and progress via a number of media and events.

Chart no. 9: Communicating quality management

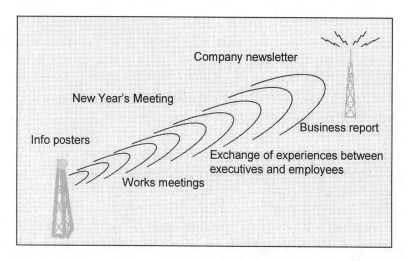

On a regular basis, the employees receive information relating to the quality management procedure in order to keep them up-to-date on progress, and changes and to emphasize the significance this process

has for Haspa. The contents of this information vary from an introduction to specific topics, or highlighting success stories of
individual branches and service centers, to the findings of Mystery
Shopping and customer satisfaction surveys. The aim of communicating this information - apart from purely conveying them - is to
achieve a higher level of transparency with regard to the activities
relating to quality that are taking place within the organization. This
approach is intended to help perceive quality as something that
comes naturally, not as something extraordinary.

4.5 Future prospects

Since 1993, quality management has become an established part of
Haspa; apart from the Quality Teams, measuring quality in branches
and service centers has played a role of utmost importance in this
development. The branches and service centers are the places where
the quality management procedure is filled with life, due to the links
with other activities geared towards the marketplace.

Not all of the departments at the heart of the organization, i.e. those
without direct contact with the customers, have scrutinized the issue
of quality as closely as those interfacing with the customers. The
reason for this is surely the difficulty of perceiving their own
colleagues as "genuine" internal customers who have the same needs
regarding friendliness, reliability and helpfulness like external
customers. Definite plans to implement further initiatives to
facilitate an increase in the quality of services in back office departments are already being discussed. These plans take the expectations
of the branches and service centers into account and aim at increasing quality awareness.

In addition to this, with regard to the process of setting targets, the
extent to which the Personnel Development And Leadership
Objectives, as well as the Objectives For Personal Development, can
be applied as factors of the variable benefits system in order to determine bonuses, is currently being discussed.

Generally speaking, the quality management process is subject to permanent re-evaluation. The aim is to continuously adapt to the changing requirements of the customers and to move ahead in unison with other changes in progress, towards a continuous increase in quality.

5 Measuring organizational commitment in merging companies with NFO TRI*M

Enno Walther

Both life science and especially the plant protection industry have been and are still undergoing a very dynamic consolidation process by merging entire worldwide active companies or specific sectors of business units of such global organizations.

A specific example hereof is the recent process of forming a global plant protection/ production group in several strategic steps by first merging the agrochemical divisions of Schering and Hoechst forming AgrEvo in 1998 and subsequently followed by merging the agrochemical units of AgrEvo and Rhône Poulenc into Aventis CropScience in 2000. The latter being a part of the overall merger of the life science activities of Hoechst and Rhône Poulenc in 2000. This report refers only to experiences made in measuring by NFO TRI*M the development of the organizational commitment worldwide during the merger phases of the respective agrochemical and biotech sectors of the above mentioned companies finally forming an organization resulting in plant protection and plant growth companies ranging under the first 2 to 3 world market leaders.

5.1 NFO TRI*M Employee Commitment survey in AgrEvo 1998 ("dialogue & actions")

Objectives

The project has been developed and run by a small empowered interfunctional project team fully supported by the board, the regional and country management and approved by the labour representative bodies before launching.Thus this project was accepted throughout the organization from the very beginning. The survey was held in 24 different languages in 120 countries where the new group has had business activities. In AgrEvo "dialogue &actions" (nomen est omen) focussed mainly on the following objectives:

As a pre-condition for taking action it was decided to measure worldwide the organizational commitment 3 years after the merger of the agrochemical divisions of Hoechst and Schering in order to identify the major strengths and weaknesses at all hierarchical levels in all organizational units worldwide with impact on commitment and thus the performance of the organization. The statistical appendix of the questionnaire (4 questions) was designed in a way to evaluate findings along the new organizational structure/ management responsibilities of the new company such as a global company and corporate functions, regions, individual countries and their given organizational units (minimum size 10 questionnaires returned).

By following the organizational chart it was possible to establish both findings for almost all organizational units and to generate aggregation of findings for potential specific analyses along different national, regional or global management processes both vertically and cross-functionally. Although the organizational patterns of the new company had been implemented already it has been very helpful as a secondary effect in not a few units to establish actual and comprehensive organizational charts and relate manpower to these units for other managerial purposes as well.

This highly work intensive administration of the database of the population has been recognized not only as a factor of statistical relevance for this survey but at the same time proved to be a pre-condition for the acceptance and relevance of the specific survey results by both staff and management of the units. This indispensable significant input paid fully off in the subsequent process of defining and implementing improvement measures at all above mentioned levels being the core objective of the survey.

Top management from the very beginning confirmed personally to all employees throughout the various internal media that the findings will be fully communicated and that managers at all respective levels will analyse and discuss the results for their area of responsibility with their staff personally in order to take specific action to reduce detected weaknesses and to foster strengths to improve the overall performance of the organization. Labour and management representatives fully identified with these core objectives and thus very positively supported the project through all its phases.

The commitment to these objectives, the full support of all involved plus a comprehensive communication policy for running the survey and for cascading findings and reporting on actions through personal presentations and printed and electronic media made it possible to achieve the additional overall objective which was to initiate a sustainable bottom-up process for dialogue and change between staff and managers at all levels. This was only possible since it was based on reliable results to develop the organisation and business according to the strategic principles for organizational development.

Benefits

When developing the concept the project team had some uncertainties whether a unique and rather long questionnaire structured in the specific NFO TRI*M Methodology would be sufficiently accepted in an organization which just underwent substantial changes. Due to the intensive communication on the objectives of the project and on the TRI*M Methodology by a comprehensive leaflet attached to the questionnaire and due to the fact that the TRI*M Methodology supplies reliable and even comparable data in even very different companies and national cultures the management and the project team were very satisfied with an achieved response rate of 71% (global average). This high response rate proved that the questions asked were accepted as very relevant worldwide and shows that employees are highly interested in their involvement in the change process as part of developing the corporate culture.

Even more significant for the objective to take actions it became clear when cascading the findings that they were regarded as realistic, important and clearly focussed to take prioritised actions. When the global findings were first communicated the overall opinion was that it would have been better to have run the survey in the very beginning of the merger process in order to steer the integration process more supported by focussed realistic survey results than by assumptions on hypothetical factors with impact on commitment. The detailed analysis of backgrounds and reasons for concrete findings and the definition of improvement measures (from management processes to day-to-day-issues) took place without delay throughout the global company. It was essential that this most important phase of the project was continuously promoted and supported by both top management and labour representatives. At the same time staff increasingly pulled for face-to-face discussion to develop jointly solutions for improving revealed weaknesses at all levels.

The best compliment for the project is the fact that it in many areas achieved to initiate an ongoing dialogue between management and staff which was even better in those areas (e.g. Supply Chain) where some scepticism existed on the factual benefits of such a survey.

Overall, one could state that both management and staff appreciate NFO TRI*M as a tool to enhance performance, to benchmark and to support developing a new corporate culture at both national and international levels.

5.2 M&A Commitment Survey in Aventis CropScience in 2000

From the experience that it would have been better to have run the organizational commitment survey in AgrEvo not only in the 3rd year after its formation but right at the beginning of the integration process the new joint top management of AgrEvo and Rhône Poulenc Agro defined even during the negotiation phase for the merger to implement a similar project to be held right after closing to mainly support the integration process from its very beginning. A small joint project team with representatives from AgrEvo and Rhône Poulenc Agro was set up to prepare for and to kick of the global M & A Commitment survey right after closing in a fully new uncertain environment in order to support the merger of equals joining two global organizations with rather different national (e.g. headquarter in Germany and France) and different company cultures as such.

In order to meet the overall goal to create a new organic company culture the objective for the NFO TRI*M project (named "Integration Barometer") focussed on providing top management of Aventis CropScience with representative information on the quality of the integration process during the first year after closing to enhance company culture by specific measures to be quickly defined and implemented.

In such a scenario it was necessary to monitor the acceptance of, the identification with and the commitment to the integration process worldwide during the first year of the new company to enhance its success and avoid major cultural clashes as strategic success factors for the merger. This was even more crucial since both agrochemical units - AgrEvo and Rhône Poulenc Agro had realized major changes during the last 3 to 4 years prior to this following new merger into Aventis CropScience.

To steer both quality and speed of the integration process top down it became a demand to benchmark its quality both internally and externally by NFO TRI*M Indices. It was made clear that it should be a first priority task for top management at global, regional or national level to implement and monitor improvement measures at these levels from the respective findings.

Top management fully identified themselves with this project and kept the promise to take necessary action derived from the aggregated findings which were promised to be communicated and discussed with management and with staff as a mainly top down management process.

Another difference to the survey in AgrEvo was that this new merger survey was not held among the whole population of the new company but was designed as a series of 3 representative samples of about 5,000 employees each taken from the worldwide organization. It was an important task to set up these samples according to the brand-new organizational structure. Although valid new organigramms did not exist at the starting point at all levels, highly intensive cooperation between the project team and the HR network throughout the company made it possible to establish a reliable database for representative sampling. Again the input made into the resulting database was an important document for many other uses within HR when shaping the new organization globally.

The samples were taken in 100 countries along the national, regional and functional organizational structure to be representative at these levels themselves as well as within the global aggregations to be made. The questionnaires were distributed in 20 languages.

The timing for the 3 samples were:

- First sample at closing (commitment at starting point).

- Second sample when the new organization had been defined (about 6 months later at the point when individuals had clarity about their new job and related structure).

- Third sample was planned for another 6 months later (measuring commitment after experience in the new organization/ culture).

The sample structure changed periodically, each employee was selected once from the representatively designed database. The project team and NFO Infratest had decided not to hold pre-consequent "full" surveys but to go for 3 samples of 5,000 each in order to avoid feelings of "over surveying" due to the short intervals of the 3 samples.

The questionnaire was identical for the 3 samples (enabling comparisons) and fully focussed on aspects indicating the quality of the integration process to make it possible to analyse during the first year after closing how both its quality and its speed are perceived and to have a solid basis for prompt necessary intervention by top management (steering the integration process was the mere top management task!). From the positive experience with NFO TRI*M in AgrEvo and standard employee surveys in Rhône Poulenc Agro staff was very open and willing to participate in the survey. Nevertheless it was essential to accompany the project by intensive marketing and communication taking into account that the survey was held in a brand new organization with many unclarities, uncertainties and fears.

Benefits

Originally there was uncertainty whether a NFO TRI*M survey would be accepted in an "unstable" global organization, but they were not confirmed at all. With more than 60% response rate (global average) in each sample wave, the tool itself, its questionnaire and its objectives were highly appreciated to give feedback to management during the crucial first year where basic patterns for the new corporate culture have to be implemented otherwise there is a risk that they will be lost.

The findings at global, regional, country and functional level gave a clear pattern of strengths and weaknesses in order to define and quickly implement measures to improve the quality of the integration process at its specific path. NFO TRI*M findings fully enabled to do so despite significant differences between the company cultures of former AgrEvo and Rhône Poulenc Agro and despite national differences in responding to survey questionnaires. On the other hand the NFO TRI*M database offered the opportunity to benchmark both quality and speed, both within units of the new corporation as well as with similar external M&A processes of other organizations. The survey results were accepted as highly relevant by management and staff to take speedy focussed action to steer it at all levels in the desired way. As a result major organizational changes related to structures and processes were promptly initiated and continued to be implemented throughout the integration phases based on the 3 samples diagnosises. The management tool "Integration Barometer" specifically supported to speed up the process to clarify and finetune the strategy of the new company and thus enhanced the speed of integration as one of the major success criteria for the merger.

6 Setting up a Customer Retention System for a major bank in Germany

Michael Schroth

6.1 Introduction

During the past years, banks and savings banks in Germany have been facing fundamental changes with regard to retail banking, and this will probably become even more dramatic in the years to come. 15 years ago, it was almost commonplace to talk of a seller's market when referring to the banking sector. However, the financial market today is close to advancing to a prototype of a buyer's market. This is especially due to the fact that products have become inter-changeable to a relatively high degree. The rapid development of information technology presents another reason for that.

These changes will pose very big challenges to financial institutions in the next years, particularly with regard to the strategies relating to sales and communication channels.

As these developments are taking their due course, an actually very old and almost trivial business principle is becoming increasingly important: a business development that is profitable in the long run can only be accomplished with (very) satisfied customers. This means customers who are convinced of the fact that their bank offers them the best products and services with regard to their financial affairs. As a consequence, the company that succeeds in establishing a close and long-term relationship with their customers, fulfils the best conditions for being successful. This is even more important in a marketplace where new competitors from related, or even completely different industries, join those competitors who look back upon a long tradition in the marketplace – and this applies to a high degree to the market of financial services.

The bank's assets, which count at the end of the day, are not primarily those registered on the balance sheet. They rather relate to the fact that customers have been successfully retained.

This also explains why the topic "Customer Relationship Management" has recently become increasingly popular with banks and savings banks.

When it comes to the medium- and long-term objectives of a bank, it is essential to add so-called "soft" factors like customer satisfaction, to monetary factors such as turnover and profit, thus creating decisive factors for customer retention. This serves the purpose to accomplish a really successful relationship management that is aiming for high-level customer satisfaction and retention. However, this should not only be verbally implied, but, if possible, be documented in such a way that each employee will be able to comprehend what the concept of relationship management is actually based upon.

The reason why this is so important lies in the fact that a management factor like customer satisfaction has to be as binding as possible. Otherwise the resulting improvements will neither be accepted nor realized. Only once this precondition has been fulfilled, can it be assumed that this issue will meet its due acknowledgement and support from decision-makers and their teams.

This is of extreme importance for the implementation and particularly for the acceptance and realization, with regard to the findings of an information and management system for customer satisfaction and retention. All managers in the marketing or sales department will only follow up those factors in greater depth on which they themselves are measured.

It goes without saying that such an information and management system has to be based on indisputable methods. Furthermore, it must have been tested and refined to a degree that would not leave any doubts as to its practical application – *conditio sine qua non*, so to speak. However methodically and scientifically efficient and practical the system may be, it will be doomed to vanish in less time than it actually took to set it up if it is not being acknowledged as binding, or accepted by the sales staff or employees in the different bank branches. This, of course, would also be nonsensical from an economical point of view since its set-up incurs considerable costs.

The Commerzbank is one of the banks that have taken up the issue of customer satisfaction at a very early stage, and integrated it as an important management factor into their guidelines as binding, and documented this accordingly. In addition to this, customer satisfaction has become a determinant for evaluating the professional ability and, subsequently, measuring the variable factors influencing the payment of executives who work in the bank's sales department.

Until the beginning of the 90's, the development of an information and management system was not really that intensely focused on. At that time, the idea of looking into the issue of customer satisfaction in a more systematic and profound way gained shape. After some research and after the first rough ideas had been collected, intense discussions about the structure of such a survey took place with several market research companies that had, amongst other things, specialized in conducting customer satisfaction studies. Finally, we decided to work with the TRI*M-System of NFO Infratest.

Nevertheless, when setting up such an information and management system it is useful to proceed in several consecutive steps. Even during the early stages, it became apparent that this system also had to be adapted to the individual sales units in order to receive the acceptance it depends on with regard to the branch network. We were also aware of the fact that - for financial reasons - the system had to be firstly developed, set up, tested and then introduced and extended in a way to keep a general overview. During the process of introducing such an information and management system, adaptations, extensions and changes have to be continually taken into account during the subsequent stages of implementation - despite its utterly thorough and elaborate conception. It is mainly the employees involved who have to learn gradually how to handle such

60

a system. That is why the process took four to five years until the system and all its components fulfilled the original idea we had of it.

Today we have established an information and management system for controlling customer satisfaction and retention that consists of several individual components (see illustration 1) and is integrated into a comprehensive quality management concept. By now, the decision-makers in the headquarters and the sales representatives in the different branches have accepted the system. Nevertheless, it would be presumptuous to claim that this system was complete or even perfect. We continually come across aspects that can be extended or improved. However, this is also due to the dynamic changes that take place in the marketplace. These also require permanent adaptations and changes with regard to marketing and sales activities.

Chart no. 1: The overall system

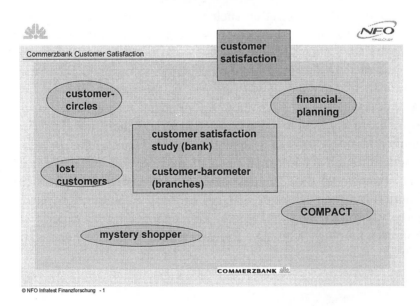

Customer satisfaction surveys on behalf of the bank as a whole and its individual branches, present the core of our information and management system. In addition to this, two product-specific surveys, as well as a survey of former customers who are using other banks, by now have taken shape during the course of time. Two very important additional concepts have resulted from the developing stage. One of them is the so-called customer forum. Another addition that is certainly of as much importance was the introduction and integration of "Mystery Shopping" into this information system, which we established three years ago.

6.2 Essential components and concept

In the following part, I would like to describe the essential components in more detail with regard to the concept they are based on and the implementation.

First it was necessary with regard to our information and management system to develop ideas about target groups, sample quotas, the technical and organizational handling, interviewing methods and, of course, the contents of the surveys. By means of a gradual procedure we intended to firstly concentrate on a study that would be representative for the bank as a whole. We did not want to proceed to the next stage, i.e. looking at results at branch level before the first stage had been realized in a promising way. The reason for that lay primarily in the fact that exceedingly higher costs would have gone along with that.

In order to obtain representative results for the bank as a whole, data tolerance range should not surpass a certain magnitude that, for example, would render a reasonable comparison between waves impossible. We intended to secure a sample that clearly ranged above 2000 respondents. This magnitude took into consideration that we would still get a meaningful sample basis even if we differentiated between the usual private customers and those customers who enjoy an elevated status. And we wanted to be able to accomplish this as well with the new system.

Regarding the interviewing method, we decided for the self-completion survey. For financial reasons, a face-to-face survey was out of the question, along with the extension to branch level we had planned for a later stage. We did not like the idea of a telephone survey on account of the very delicate matter of data protection (passing on addresses to the respective call-center of the institution) and the bank customers' extreme sensitivity with regard to this problem. However, from the financial point of view, the telephone survey would have presented an attractive alternative to the self-completion survey.

Based on the experience we can look back upon today – and, with regard to this specific instrument upon which we have only been able to accumulate our insights during the course of years – a response rate of about 15-17% can be assumed for such a self-completion survey for customers. However, this percentage can oscillate between 10 and 25% for sub-groups. This relatively wide margin proves to be realistic if you have a look at particular target groups, for example. As a matter of fact, retail customers who enjoy a more elevated status, or retail customers who have a more intensified relationship with the bank in general, are more likely to participate than the average private customer. Moreover, those customers who use our bank as their main bank tend to take part more often than customers who only consider us to be a secondary bank relationship. However, it is the latter group we have to focus on with regard to the future for they still present an enormous potential for every bank. Therefore, the sample choice resulted from a random selection of aggregated data that had been evaluated in a consecutive step.

Although this is not a new insight, it is a very relevant fact regarding market research that is often not taken into consideration enough: a shorter, optically appealing questionnaire has a positive impact on the response rate of a self-completion survey. The response rate can still be improved by offering incentives. During the course of time, the following variant has proven to be most appropriate, also with regard to the financial aspects that go along with it:

Among all participants, those respondents whose returned questionnaires we have received first, are entitled to a little "thank-you gift". In addition to that, all returned questionnaires take part in a draw where participants stand the chance to win three very attractive holidays.

Admittedly, this procedure would not work unless the respondents additionally reveal their address. This had a restricting impact on the number of returned questionnaires at first. However, we have solved this problem in a quite satisfactory fashion, namely by providing an additional sheet for the respondent's name and address, which is to be returned together with the completed questionnaire in an envelope provided. The reason why there have never been any considerable problems from the customers' side lies in the following fact: The envelope is sent to an independent market research company. The respondents have also received a letter in which it is clearly explained (in addition to the general information relating to data protection) that the address sheet will be immediately separated from the questionnaire as soon as the envelope arrives at the market research company.

Here I would like to hint at another problem regarding the response rate we specifically encountered when the survey was conducted at branch level. When we were setting up the sample we needed for that purpose, we had to exclude certain customers from the start. For example estate accounts, i.e. accounts whose legal capacity expires due to the death of the account holder, non-performing loans, banking accounts kept by a notary public in his own name for a third party on a trust basis etc. So the basic sample size has essentially decreased, especially with regard to sub-groups (e.g. high-income customers). Although the original idea was to interview a customer only once in two years, it now turned out that we could not keep up the quota we were aiming for with regard to the gross sample size we required for the surveys on branch level for some sub-groups. That is why it is possible that a customer might already be interviewed again in the following year. However, this caused some customers to refuse and, subsequently, reduced the response rate.

The actual conception of the questionnaire also posed some problems. It was less the lack of issues and wordings but rather the aim to be brief and precise. On the one hand, we were keen to obtain as much information as we could from customers regarding certain issues. Of course, another important driver in this context was the endless craving for information shown by the colleagues who are active in the most diverse groups and areas of retail banking. On the other hand, though, the experienced market researcher is aware of the fact that any extension of the questionnaire for a self-completion survey decreases the willingness to complete it. That is why we had to come to an appropriate compromise – to include as many questions as necessary, but to be as brief as possible.

Based on our experience with handling this instrument, we can say that less is often more. The degree to which the instrument will be accepted, especially later on branch level, also depends on the clear layout and straightforwardness of the results. Thus, it has not only had a positive effect on the percentage of returned questionnaires, but also on the acceptance and realization to focus on the central questions relating to the issues customer satisfaction and retention.

It is an essential function of the questionnaire to determine the importance and performance of the most crucial quality components from the customers' point of view. "Having to complete the very same criteria twice" naturally takes up some space, but it is an indispensable means of analysis for allocating priorities with regard to the realization. As this part of the questionnaire represents the core of both the survey and the TRI*M system, it was inevitable that there was only limited space for other issues or questions. In spite of the limited space available for the questionnaire, we have been able to incorporate all the questions that are required by the TRI*M system, and relevant from our point of view.

The first survey, i.e. the pilot wave for the bank as a whole, hardly met any problems when it was conducted. The sample was internally selected through a program that randomly generates numbers. The mail-out including a letter, the four-page questionnaire and the prepaid envelope was produced by our in-house print shop (at this stage, incentives were not used yet; therefore there was no need for an additional address sheet). The dispatch unit of Commerzbank took care of sending everything out. The returned questionnaires were directly passed on to NFO Infratest Munich.

As already mentioned earlier, the first wave was launched without incentives. As a matter of fact, the estimated response rate did not quite meet our expectations. Anyway, we were able to increase the return quota distinctly by offering incentives for the following waves.

Minor problems (e.g. incorrect addresses) arose with regard to the addresses the mail-outs were supposed to be sent to. It became once again apparent what used to cause trouble with regard to previous sales mail-outs: the address directory is not always being kept up-to-date with appropriate care and priority. With regard to this, more cost-effective procedures could be implemented that would also prevent negative customer responses. However, we were able to tackle the problem in a more efficient manner: on the one hand by insisting on establishing and extending the management of a customer database, which lead to the more thorough handling of address data; on the other hand, by implementing corresponding programs for comparing addresses. The problem though, could not be completely solved.

The results of this first survey of the bank as a whole, provided us with much insight. Except for the general insight into the degree of our customers' satisfaction and, of course, dissatisfaction, the importance of individual service components and their evaluation presented a very essential and partly astonishing piece of information. For some service components, the results - with regard to both their importance and their evaluation - met our range of expectations. However, as far as the one or the other criterion was concerned, we were actually taken by surprise, particularly regarding their relevance with respect to customer satisfaction.

Although relating price-related aspects do play an important role, they are not the most decisive factor with regard to customer retention. Factors like expertise, meeting the customers' needs in an individualized and active manner, and courtesy, have proven to be far more relevant drivers.

As a consequence, the classification of factors that are of ultimate importance with regard to customer satisfaction, mainly names the so-called motivators. Amongst them are factors that have been standardized ("Hygienics"). There are also factors that have not been relevant with regard to customer satisfaction up to now. However, they could become so in the near future ("Hidden Opportunities"). Last but not least, the classification also lists factors that contribute less to customer satisfaction at the moment ("Potential Savers"). From our point of view, this classification is very useful and valuable as far as the realization and allocation of priorities is concerned.

However, there have been two serious information deficits recently that struck us as evenly important. Admittedly, the results we achieved provided us with the percentage of customers who were completely satisfied, very satisfied or even dissatisfied. They kept us informed about the most important issues their degree of satisfaction related to and how we were rated there. However, we lacked a direct instrument for comparing these results with other banking institutes.

The second flaw - but we were already aware of it from the beginning – lay in the fact that the result of the survey of the bank as a whole only provided an average evaluation of Commerzbank as such. This means that well performing branches could compensate for branches whose performance was not rated as satisfying. This led to an averagely satisfying result that did not show where there could be any flaws that might have been overlooked due to this leveling effect. However, without conducting the survey on branch level it will hardly be possible to find out which branches do not perform that well, or even to prove anything in that respect. If in doubt, any manager will stick to the principle: the poorly performing branches are always the branches run by other managers.

How big the differences are, can actually be seen by the fact that the results for customer satisfaction as we collected them in the second stage, vary a lot from branch to branch.

Chart no. 2 : Spread and range of TRI*M

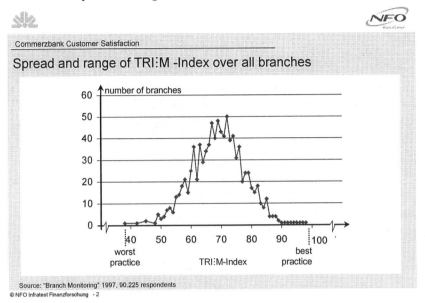

Although we did not have any documented evidence of this insight before the introduction of the branch survey, we had known beforehand that a customer satisfaction study on the level of the bank as a whole would provide interesting and informative results. We were also aware of the fact that it would give us some indication for comprehensive and general improvements. However, the approach that would finally play the most important role with regard to improvements in the context of customer satisfaction could only be realized when weaknesses were identified on a local level – it is a well-known fact that "all business is local".

In the case of a bank like the Commerzbank, we are dependent on our branches when it comes to business activities and success because customer satisfaction and retention is mostly based on the personal experiences the customer associates with his or her local branch. From the customer's point of view, Commerzbank is not the headquarters, the Frankfurt skyscraper with its thousands of employees, or the total of all branches. From the customer's point of view, Commerzbank is primarily his or her local branch with its employees. As a matter of fact, customers who are situated in Munich experience Commerzbank in a different way from customers in Hamburg.

The Commerzbank adheres to certain Corporate Identity guidelines with regard to design. That is why each Commerzbank branch follows the same basic style when it comes to decoration. However, the branches do differ from each other as far as their environment, façade and the architecture of the interior are concerned. All this has a different impact on customers. At the end of the day, the most decisive factor with regard to customer satisfaction is the employee or the team that works in a branch. Needless to say that the employees in Hamburg are different from those you might deal with in Munich even if they happen to work for the same company.

We found quite an elegant solution to eliminate the first weakness, i.e. setting up a benchmarking tool. For almost 30 years, NFO Infratest has established FMDS ("Financial Market Data Service"). Each year, characteristic structural data of the financial market is collected based on large sample sizes, with all well-known banks, savings banks, insurances and building societies represented. After some discussions with clients, questions on the respondents' (customers') satisfaction with their own bank and three more TRI*M questions (recommendation, continuation of business relationship and competitive advantage) were integrated into the FMDS system. This is the reason why a comparison with other banks is possible and our own results can be interpreted accordingly.

It was quite easy to accomplish this since other financial institutions had also begun to set up customer satisfaction studies in a more systematic way and were equally interested in having a standardized means for comparing banks.

It was considerably harder to solve the second problem – the branch survey that had been acknowledged as an indispensable option beforehand. The essential problem we were facing with regard to that was the cost factor.

In order to have acceptable results within the branch network, it is necessary to provide representative results with justifiable data tolerance range (i.e. comparisons of different waves as well as comparisons of different branches). Therefore, we need a sufficient sample size for each branch. Without applying any higher math, it became apparent that we would rapidly reach a 6-figure DM sum at the top end with the sample we needed for 1000 branches. Naturally, this meant that we had to face an enormous cost factor.

That is why, at first, we considered taking this part of the customer satisfaction into our own hands. However, during the course of the further development this only proved to be a partly useful and cost-saving procedure. The cost for sending mail-outs, especially the postage, presented the biggest problem or cost factor with regard to such a sample size.

An average Commerzbank branch consists of a little more than 3000 customers. On this basis, we had set 100 completes as the lowest limit we required. Taking the response rate of the survey of the bank as a whole into account, we could well assume that we needed to send a total of 800,000 mail-outs. It was necessary to reduce this amount considerably by applying adequate measures and to generate a response rate as high as possible.

One of the options was to cut down on the size of the questionnaire, which helps to increase the respondents' willingness to participate. With regard to the branch survey, we decided to omit one part of the questionnaire, i.e. the questions relating to importance. We assumed that there were not any significant differences among the individual branches. This had already become evident by the analysis of the survey for the bank as a whole.

As a consequence, the branch survey questionnaire just contained questions regarding the satisfaction with different aspects that relate to the performance of the local branch – and this was the most important thing. However, the questions relating to importance were still part of the sample for the survey of the bank as a whole. This was also the most decisive reason for carrying on with the survey of the bank as a whole, as the total of branch surveys already represents the bank as a whole. Moreover, some more questions that more or less related to the bank as a whole could be omitted from the branch survey. As a result, we were able to concentrate the questionnaire for this survey onto two pages – the front and back of one DIN A 4 sheet. In addition to that, the weight of the mail-out was reduced, which was also relevant with regard to the postage.

Chart No. 3

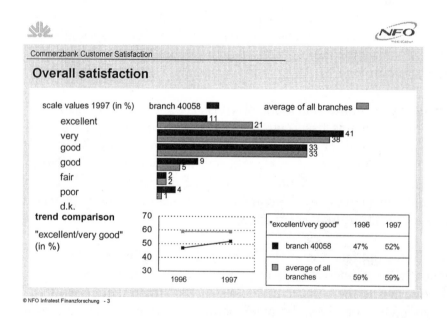

The issue "incentives" presented the second essential factor for increasing the percentage of returned questionnaires and, subsequently, decreasing the total number of mail-outs. We have been trying several variants over the years, for example: altruistic or egotistic prices. Finally, with regard to cost-effectiveness, rewarding three attractive holidays as well as the small thank-you gift for the first 1000 surveys that have been returned turned out to be the most powerful incentives. By which means, we were able to increase the percentage of returned questionnaires to well over 15% (for specific sub-groups to even more than 20%); in accordance to that, we were also able to reduce the total number of mail-outs.

As far as the branch survey was concerned, we also set up the sample, had the letters and questionnaires printed in-house and sent out by our own dispatch unit – a total of 600,000 mail-outs. The questionnaires that were returned for the first wave went directly to Commerzbank. An external data entry provider was commissioned to enter the questionnaire data and provided us with a complete SPSS file. Then an employee of our market research department dealt with the actual statistical evaluation in SPSS. In a further step, all the results were translated into PowerPoint charts. Thus, we accomplished the evaluation of each branch individually and set up reports on the questions that had been asked.

However, two things have become apparent since the first wave of the branch survey. First of all, even if handling such comprehensive and extensive information presents a manageable task, it is very time and energy consuming for an employee who is not used to dealing with such matters on a daily basis; especially as this is supposed to be accomplished in a way that would meet the high professional standards of a market research company that specializes in these things. The lower resourced companies who are prepared to provide for internal market research, represent another obstacle that has to be overcome in this context. Due to the less refined degree of expertise (that is based on several persons and teams in a market research company, anyway) and equipment, the outcome of this procedure did not turn out to be as professional with regard to the results as it would have been with a market research company.

As a result of very intense discussions with the market research company, we found a solution for the following years that helped us to improve on that issue and seemed acceptable from the financial point of view. However, with the considerable success of this instrument that could already be detected during the initial stage, the willingness to put up with a certain level of cost also increased. For this reason, the gradual procedure has paid off as well. Today, the branch survey works like the survey for the bank as a whole: Commerzbank takes the sample and uses their in-house resources for printing and sending of the mail-outs. NFO Infratest takes care of the returned questionnaires, the questionnaire data entry, coding, evaluation and translation of the results into tables, excel sheets and graphic charts.

The only difference between the survey of the bank as a whole and the branch survey lies in the fact that the survey of the bank as a whole contains the total number of aspects on importance and the survey of the bank as a whole takes place every two years. The reason for that is due to the fact that importance and meaning of performance criteria change in an increasingly rapid manner and, therefore, have to be accordingly adapted within our information system. The branch survey is launched on an annual base as it also lays the foundation for the annual evaluation of the branch employees' performance and the calculation of the percentage of their bonus or royalty every year.

I would like to take this opportunity for a brief digression on how the results of the studies are being used in the context of our system of objectives and the performance orientated payment that is related to it.

For some years, Commerzbank has linked parts of variable payment, such as bonus percentages, with the fulfillment of specific criteria. Important criteria in the area of sales are, of course, factors that are relevant to the profit, for example, the turnover. In addition to that, there are also structural objectives that primarily serve the medium- and long-term management of a certain business area. One of these structural factors is customer satisfaction. Thus, during the annual objectives talks, for example, an agreement on a specific magnitude relating to the improvement of customer satisfaction will be accomplished together with the branch manager. At the end of the period of time that has been settled for the assessment, the question as to whether the agreed magnitude has been fulfilled, also has some impact on the amount of the bonus percentage.

In addition to that, the bank has emphasized and internally communicated that the issue of customer satisfaction is a pivotal component of the company concept and, as a consequence, a central business objective in the last year. This was the outcome of intense workshops. As a result, the importance of customer satisfaction has become such a prominent factor within the company guidelines that it has become absolutely impossible for any decision maker not to take it into consideration when making his or her plans.

Apart from the fact that its corporation in business objectives and performance-related pay has rendered customer satisfaction a crucial factor, its potential for the practical realization of the results is also of outstanding importance with regard to its acceptance in the area of sales. For that reason, we have not only concentrated on the analysis and representation of the results. In addition, we have provided the branches with helpful means for realizing these results. Hence each branch receives a visually appealing report after the analysis has been concluded because, due to the enormous flux of internal information, designing also plays an important role within the company.

First, the report shows the most important results of the bank as a whole compared to its competitors – an overview of the entire market, so to speak. In the following part the results are depicted as relating to the individual branches and compared to the bank as a whole. In addition to that, they are also compared to the top ten branches ("best practice") by means of figures, graphic charts along a time line.

By use or these results, individual branches can identify their specific strengths and weaknesses with regard to the criteria relevant to customer satisfaction. They can also view their performance in comparison to other branches (average performance, "best practice"). At the end of this part, a summary of the strengths and weaknesses documents everything at a glance.

The next part of the report contains a set of forms. Here the percentage that shows how low a branch actually ranges below the average has to be entered once again for each performance criterion that has been rated worse than the average of the bank as a whole. Presumable reasons for the situation can be given from the branch's point of view. There is also room for indicating the measures that have been introduced for eliminating respective weaknesses, for the time frame within which the improvements should be accomplished and which member of staff at the branch is responsible for this.

One could come up with the objection, though, that at first glance this might be a very formalistic approach, especially from the creative marketing person's point of view. However, looking back on years and years of practical work, I have come to learn that it is these things in particular, a lot of employees "cling to" when it comes to the realization of such a system. That is why there should be relatively binding regulations for the practical handling of such results and their realization towards a certain direction. This would provide the people in charge with a tool that would help them to get orientated with regard the realization of the results. This has nothing to do with enforcing formalistic ideas. Rather, it ensures homogeneous procedures and also helps the quality control department to evaluate both the measures that have been applied and their success.

As far as the measures that should be taken are concerned it is also useful to offer corresponding support to the sales department. For this reason our branch report contains a chapter in the following paragraph in which potential measures are described for the different performance criteria. We use various sources for elaborating this so-called catalogue of measures.

We used to develop the catalogue of measures – after the second year of the branch survey – with sales employees in internal workshops by discussing the potential reasons for customer dissatisfaction and corresponding solutions for individual performance criteria. These discussions were based on the experience of our employees. Due to the fact that our sales representatives were very knowledgeable about their customers' needs, this presented a sufficient basis at first. Nevertheless, we thought that, at length, this approach lacked the customers' original point of view as the sales persons' position is always subject to extraneous influences in one way or another.

That is why at this point, we decided to organize "customer forums". We developed a guideline for further discussion that we based on the performance criteria covered by the customer satisfaction surveys. This guideline was to shed light on these individual criteria from the customer's point of view by focusing on one important aspect after the other. Thus, the criterion "waiting periods", for example, was discussed under the aspect of when, or under what circumstances customers get annoyed with waiting periods in order to introduce measures for improvement that will meet the customers specific needs. In this case it turned out that customers do not always feel that longer waiting periods are annoying. However, the results are different when customers notice that waiting periods occur because bank employees, who could prevent such a situation from arising, occupy themselves with other things. This means that waiting periods do meet the customer's expectations if they occur within reasonable bounds. But this will only be the case if the customer feels that all the employees available at the time take care of the customers and are keen to reduce the waiting periods for the customers to a minimum degree.

As a result, all the performance criteria covered by the original questionnaire were discussed during the customer forums.

At that time we came to acknowledge once again, the fact that customer forums or group discussions are an excellent means to analyze the customer's disposition and attitudes towards certain issues, such as customer satisfaction in a more thorough and comprehensive way than we would have been able to accomplish by means of a standardized questionnaire. That is why they represent an ideal addition to the standardized interview - especially with regard to a relatively emotional issue such as customer satisfaction. In the future, we will view customer forums as an appropriate option – in the sense of the "voice of the customer", that is - for analyzing issues that go beyond customer satisfaction or for updating the discourse of the performance criteria associated with customer satisfaction from time to time.

The individual activities undertaken in the branches present another source for updating our catalogue of activities. As I have already mentioned before, branches fill in a checklist in which, amongst other things, appropriate activities for improving on weaknesses have been listed. Each branch sends a copy of these overviews to us. We do not take over any tasks that have to do with quality control (that would surpass our capacities in centralized market research). Instead, the next level in the organizational hierarchy above the branches (regional headquarters) covers this aspect. We simply evaluate these activities with regard to the question and whether they comprise new approaches and ideas that seem to be promising with regard to resolving the problem. If this is the case, we then incorporate them into the catalogue of activities for the whole organization. As a result, all the other branches have the chance to profit from these elaborate ideas in the following years.

Thus, each branch has a comprehensive set of tools that it can employ to detect its specific weaknesses and to decide on priorities. On the other hand, each branch has access to a large pool of ideas from which an appropriate package of activities can be customized to be implemented during the course of the following year to increase customer satisfaction.

We have handed over the authority to decide on most of the priorities to the individual branches. However, those performance criteria that are most important with regard to customer satisfaction (motivators) should always play a decisive role. Apart from that, the branches should concentrate specifically on those performance criteria of which the performance of the branch has been ranked below average in comparison to the bank as a whole. Of course, there also are the top branches whose performance have been rated above average in most or sometimes even all of the criteria. In this case the "best practice" rating, i.e. the average rating of the top ten branches, should be the set target.

By now, our customer satisfaction survey has been running for eight consecutive years. The branch-specific survey is entering its sixth year. During this period of time we have not made any major changes to the central contents; not least because we wanted to ensure cross-wave comparability. However, the information system as a whole has been constantly extended and expanded over this period of time.

Although the customer satisfaction survey was at first limited to our two target groups - private customers and individual customers - we have also been conducting the survey with our private banking customers, i.e. our top clients, for three years. To facilitate this, we had to apply some minor modification to the questionnaire, whilst, at the same time taking care to preserve comparability with the core of the general questionnaire. It has to be emphasized once again that the comparability of the data is absolutely essential with regard the acceptability of such a system.

In addition to our traditional branch system, we also included the evaluation of the Commerzbank shops into this system three years ago. These "shops" represent a specific kind of branch; they are situated within supermarkets and differ from the other branches in terms of design and equipment. Due to these various differences the questionnaire had to be slightly modified. Again, we took care not to make changes to central research questions in order to ensure comparability with other surveys.

Now that I have described the two main components of our research efforts in the context of customer satisfaction: - the survey of the bank as a whole and the branch survey - in detail, I would like to focus on three more issues for the sake of completeness: two surveys relating to specific products and the leaving customers' survey.

The surveys I have discussed so far related to customer satisfaction with Commerzbank or with local branches of Commerzbank in general. That implies that customers voice their opinions based on their experience with the bank, the employees at their local branch or any contact they have had over the phone. Hence, customers could have used several products and services or, on the other hand, could have co-operated with the bank to a much lesser extend; their views will always refer to the overall impression they have of the bank, the branch and the employees – and that is exactly what we were aiming for when we designed the questionnaire. Even if we ask about specific aspects of the bank's performance, e.g. professional competence, waiting times, or the employee's courtesy, the answers will (and should) be based on the customers' overall experience with the bank (with the most current experiences certainly playing the most important role).

Nevertheless, there are some specific products and services that are of interest and justify a focused and thorough analysis. It is probably not worthwhile designing a dedicated customer satisfaction survey for savings accounts or standardized loans; even more so, since, questions on the use of common products are integrated into our customer satisfaction survey and we therefore know which product or products the respondents refers to in their evaluations.

Among other things, Commerzbank offers comprehensive financial planning as part of their range of more complex products. This service is an exclusive product that can be purchased at a specific price and which involves various stages with diverse and comprehensive service components. Here it makes sense to focus on customer satisfaction with regard to individual product components in a more detailed manner, even more so since sales of this product are based on word of mouth.

This product appeals to a specific target group of persons with higher incomes or assets. Customers who are satisfied with this product will recommend it - as well as the bank itself, of course – to their friends and acquaintances, many of who will certainly belong to the same target group. From many market analyses, we know how important a factor of recommendation by friends and acquaintances is in banking, for attracting new customers. This aspect plays a particularly strong role in this category of products.

We also apply the TRI*M system here, i.e. we determine which product-related aspects of service are of high importance with regard to customer satisfaction. Then we analyze how the performance is rated with regard to these aspects of service in the context of the respective product. Thus, criteria like individuality, transparency, impartiality, value for money, amount of personal data collected, time taken for the analysis, helpful hints to ensure the desired results, consideration given legal, tax-related aspects and customer care provided by the account manager during the process of agreeing on a product package and after-sales care all influence the evaluation. Hence, the components of the products that can be optimized further, can be pinpointed with greater accuracy.

We are also running a similar product-related customer satisfaction survey for our product "COMPACT", which comprises standardized asset management. Due to the complexity of this product and its diverse service components, it makes sense to employ the TRI*M system for optimizing the offers according to the customers' needs.

The leaving customers' survey has become another very exciting part of our information system. Customers leave a bank for a large variety of reasons. Such a decision can be based on circumstances emanating from a person's private life, e.g. taking up residency in another area or giving up one's job. However, it is also possible that bank-related factors are the cause, for example when a loan has been paid off or the customer relationship is terminated from the bank's side. In this context, we have internal statistics consisting of the reasons for the termination of the relationship that have been recorded right away at the point where the relationship ended. Customer dissatisfaction/annoyance is also included in these statistics. Fortunately, it is hardly just one per cent of all customers who leave the bank for that reason according to these statistics – if we trust this data. In this respect, the statistics are obviously "lying". This is understandable, though, as the personal banker records the reason for termination of the relationships. Which personal banker likes to admit that one of the branch's customers has been lost due to him or her being annoyed?

Amongst other things, it was for this reason that we decided to scrutinize the reasons for customers leaving the bank in a more thorough manner - that is, directly with those persons involved. To facilitate this, we proceed as follows: we filter all the customers where we have reason to believe that the reasons for them leaving the bank have been recorded wrongly. This applies to approximately 0% of all cases. For the rest (e.g. if a builder's mortgage has been paid back), it is safe to assume that the reason for terminating the bank relationship has been recorded correctly. We then take a random sample out of these 60% and send a mail-out including a letter and freepost reply card.

Naturally you can assume that customers who have left the bank do not generally show too much willingness to sacrifice even more time to that bank. For that reason we have decided to opt for a freepost reply card. On its back, you just have to tick whether you have left the bank because you were dissatisfied or for some other reason. If it was because of dissatisfaction, they are asked to give reason for this dissatisfaction in detail. Although this was a very brief kind of interview, it fulfilled its purpose and lead to an unexpectedly high response rate of more than 20%.

As a result we were able to see that with regard to the overall number of customers who have left the bank our internal statistics deviated notably from the number of customers who have actually left the bank because they were dissatisfied. Moreover, we were provided with an overview of the most important reasons for customer dissatisfaction.

Again, we received the same feedback we had already come to expect with other customer satisfaction surveys: it is not often price-related aspects that play a decisive role, but more often the staff conduct. Hence, customer services form a crucial factor in the decision to stay with a bank or to change to another one.

6.3 Review of mystery shopping

Finally I would like to turn your attention to a more detailed review of "Mystery Shopping". Up to a certain degree, these "test purchases" represent a supplementary tool for customer satisfaction surveys. Customer satisfaction is a process that needs to be nurtured and therefore takes some time to show effects. As a general rule, however, the reverse process can be observed (i.e. a build-up in dissatisfaction) as taking place far more quickly than developments in the positive direction.

This also means that measurements that form part of the customer satisfaction surveys entail a much greater time lag when it comes to recognizing positive developments, compared to the measurement of negative tendencies. Substantial positive developments can only be recognized in mid-term and long-term analyses across several years; this even applies to changes that take place on branch-level. "Test purchases", however, make it possible to verify whether measures that have been taken to facilitate positive developments, e.g., an increase in customer satisfaction, are really being incorporated into day-to-day business; these "test purchases" can be undertaken shortly after implementing new measures.

In the past five years, we have been conducting "test purchases" in a systematic manner. In the first year, this took place in the form of a regional pilot. During the following four years, we have extended it to a national scale, i.e. covering our entire 900 plus branches. Roughly 1000 test purchases are undertaken in Commerzbank branches during the course of one year, with about 100 further test purchases from competitors. Therefore, we do not only collect information on how our own implementations have progressed, but also gain insight into how our performance compares to our competitors'.

The "test purchases" involve four sales or consulting situations: opening a current account, investing a moderate amount of money, investing a large amount of money and taking out a mortgage. For each test environment, we evaluate aspects that relate to the personal bankers' personal conduct such as courtesy, attentiveness and confidentiality, as well as focusing on essential components of a personal banker's professional expertise, e.g. scope and depth of the consultation, but also on the comprehensibility of the consultation from the "layman's" point of view. Of course, the consultation is also evaluated with regard to the specifics of the product in question, e.g. a builder's mortgage. Each tester is being assigned a specific role and calls up the branch to try to make an appointment (in the latter three of the test situations). This enables us to test our employees' behavior on the phone as well. The next step is the "test" consultation at the branch. Afterwards, the tester fills in the test consultation form. This used to take place outside the branch after the consultation.

For quite some time, we have conducted complementary feedback sessions to go with the "Mystery shopping". Now "test purchasers" reveal their identity immediately after the consultation and offer their consultants immediate feedback. The branches enthusiastically accepted this procedure, which gives us the opportunity to cover two aspects simultaneously. So we have gained additional information and a quality control mechanism. In addition, we have established what could be seen as extra training. Nevertheless, we do evaluate individual branches or even individual employees in order to ensure the personal banker's anonymity. This was one of the conditions we had to agree on in order on to get the go-ahead of the workers' council.

Generally, we have limited the accuracy of our evaluations and comparisons to the level of our 20 regional headquarters. For this reason, our management tools are to a certain extent limited with regard to exerting control beyond the regional level. However, this does not render the tool itself less appealing. We are able to discern accurately the degree to which the measures and procedures we introduced are being implemented. For instance, it becomes evident to what extent a personal banker analyses the new "customer's" situation and how he or she records this data. In addition to that – depending on the type of consultation - product specifics, e.g. the use of specific sales materials can be observed. As we evaluate certain aspects several times a year (every two months), we are able to respond within a very short time and enforce or cut down on specific measures.

The mere fact that "test purchases" are conducted throughout the whole year and that the branches are actually aware of this helps to influence the conduct of the employees in the branches in a positive way that all customers will approve of. As a result, it also has a positive impact on the customers' satisfaction with the bank. In the "test purchases", we have found an ideal supplement to our information and management system for customer satisfaction and customer retention that forms an important part of our quality management system.

7 Data Matching and Data Mining with EX•A•MINE: putting TRI*M results into immediate action

Ursula Becker, Gernot Hennig, Dr. Thomas Liehr

7.1 Market Research fills the information gap for Customer Relationship Management by means of Data Matching

Companies are conducting market research with various goals: to find out which features of a product most appeal to customers, to set a price for a new product, to discover client segments which have similar needs and attitudes. They also conduct TRI*M customer retention studies to determine which factors influence customer loyalty and how good the company's performance is with respect to the drivers of customer loyalty.

These are all very important pieces of critical information for strategic decision making in marketing. But modern companies will think of how this information could be put into action immediately: The recent trends in customer relationship management reveal an urgent need for precise and up-to-date information about the customer, no matter if the programmes are named 1:1 marketing, direct marketing or dialogue marketing. So, why not make more extensive use of market research information? The company internal data contains mainly the "hard facts" about the past buying behavior of the client, but "soft facts" like attitudes or satisfaction are generally not covered. Where would this information come from, anyway? While hard facts provide findings about the past behavior, soft facts are essential for predicting the future behavior of customers and add to a more complete picture of the customer. Market research can fill this information gap.

Let's look at some examples of how results from market research studies can be thought of as directly enabling direct marketing campaigns: Once I know that in my anonymous survey there are for example 50% of my clients are apostles, who are they? For example, if I knew this, I would immediately have a promising target group for "clients acquire clients" programmers. Or how can I find out how likely a client in my customer database is to be a rebel? This would give me good hints for estimating which clients are in danger of leaving, and thus to take actions on the profitable ones amongst them. Another example: Hostages are generally considered as "safe", but only as long as the barriers tying them to my company are in place! If I knew, which customers are likely to be of this type, targeted programmes working on the causes of dissatisfaction would help to deactivate this sleeping churn potential at times when there are still chances to act.

We see that typical customer relationship campaigns often deal with questions that neither the company internal data (demographics of clients and behavior with respect to the specific company, e.g. transactions) nor the market research data ("market-wide" behavior and attitudes) alone can answer. Only the combination of both data sources allows the company to draw conclusions about the "general" behavior and the attitudes from the transactional data which is present in a company.

The combination of these different data sources in order to gain a more realistic and holistic view of clients is called database enrichment. Literally speaking, market research information "enriches" the customer database by adding the attitudinal perspective and information about customer behavior with respect to the competitors. The methods used by NFO Infratest in order to achieve this target are referenced as Data Matching. The logic and process of Data Matching will be explained in more detail later on in this article by using a practical example. But let's first have a look at how databases are currently being used for deriving actionable knowledge about the customer relationship with Data Mining.

7.2 Internal data situation in companies: the base for Data Mining

During the past years most of the big companies have realized the need to consolidate the information they have been collecting about their clients, but this information was spread all over the company. Data Warehouses have been built which contain the information of several previously existing databases and provide access to this assembled data pool for analyzes purposes. These Data Warehouses and the increasing power of computers have encouraged companies to systematically gather even more information about their clients and their transactions than before.

Some of the new databases in Data Warehouses are even generated automatically. Electronic scanning cash registers in supermarkets, the recording of credit card transactions, as well as electronic commerce are just some examples of these databases. Fayad et al. (1996) state that "... the explosive growth of many business, government and scientific databases has far outpaced our ability to interpret and digest this data, creating a need for a new generation of tools and techniques for automated and intelligent database analysis." Companies that are already in the possession of huge databases try to analyze and exploit the data for new purposes so that the information, for example the composition of their clients, will not lie fallow but create profitable connections and new value for the company.

The only problem is what to do with these amounts of data and how to exploit them in the most beneficial manner. Buzz words which are often heard when it comes to analyzing huge quantities of data are "Data Mining" and "Knowledge Discovery in Databases".

The term "Data Mining" is frequently being used, often without knowing what Data Mining really means. It can be stated that Data Mining combines elements of statistics, computer science and databases to form a "toolbox" enabling "Knowledge Discovery" in large databases. Applications that deal with Knowledge Discovery in Databases are becoming increasingly important not only in various

88

scientific areas, but also in business settings and especially in marketing. Data Mining techniques applied by a skilled and experienced analyst help to "get the most out of your data" in terms of analytical insight.

Typical customer relationship management applications of Data Mining include e.g. optimization of target groups, identifying typical product purchase combinations via market basket analysis or predicting churn behavior. Most important when trying to build these models is an in-depth knowledge of the respective business. This certainly does not mean that technical and statistical knowledge is not needed – on the contrary it is very important – but the understanding of the real processes underlying the data is the critical condition when building effective models. This is also documented by CRISP-DM, the cross industry standard process model for Data Mining, an industry and software neutral process "template" which has emerged as the leading standard for handling and documenting Data Mining projects: CRISP-DM starts with business understanding, the data only comes second.

Chart no. 1

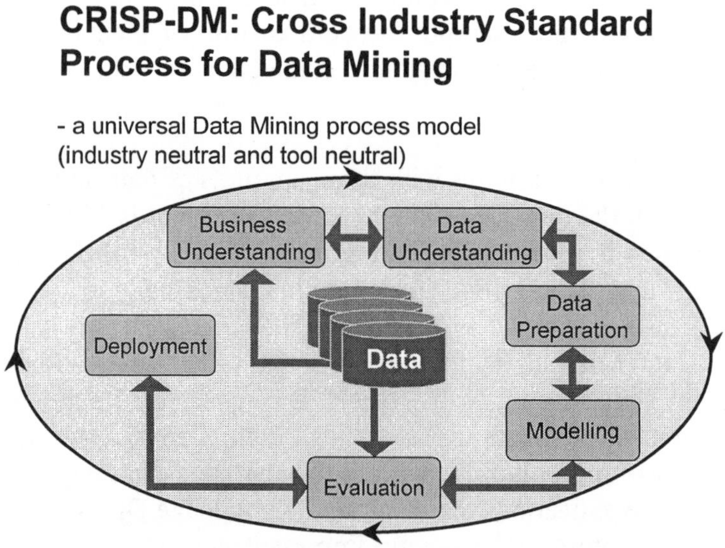

CRISP-DM: Cross Industry Standard Process for Data Mining

- a universal Data Mining process model
(industry neutral and tool neutral)

Source: CRISP-DM 1.0, Step-by-step data mining guide, http://www.crisp-dm.org

This focus on the business reality - considering the available data as an indicator for what's going on in the real world – implies also taking into account what potential information the data contains and especially where its limits are. This brings us back to the discussion of what can be derived from internal company data (mainly internal behavioral), and how market research data enhances the information content with respect to "external" behavioral and attitudinal information. Because any Data Mining model can only be as good as the information content of the data it is built upon, Data Matching for database enrichment is a crucial step in assembling relevant data. This ensures the Data Mining model makes use of all information available that could develop better models, which in turn results in reducing marketing costs due to better selected campaign target groups with for example higher response rates.

The EX▪A▪MINE toolbox handles all of the "classical" Data Mining tasks as well as the building of Data Matching models.

7.3 Data Matching enriches customer databases and improves Customer Relationship Management and "One-to-One" Marketing

The general aim of one-to-one marketing is to address each client in the best possible manner according to his or her specific situation and the individual needs of the client in order to become more customer centric. As it is very difficult and expensive to find out from every single client what is the best way to address him at every moment in time, in practice rather a "one-to-segment marketing" than "one-to-one marketing" is used. In one-to-segment marketing one identifies homogeneous segments within one's customer database. Here the term "homogeneous segments" means clients who are comparable with respect to their needs and attitudes.

The goal is then to develop marketing actions for each of these segments and to tailor these activities in the best way to the profile of the segment. The underlying assumption is, that once the segments are formed, they can be identified in the customer base. Due to data protection laws the market research results cannot be directly applied to the master data. The master data of companies

90

however consists of some demographic variables and the past behavior of the clients, but no information about attitudes and satisfaction of customers. This lack of attitudinal information about clients and their needs in the databases of companies poses an evident problem to the segmentation.

Data Matching, a proven analytical CRM based technique, helps to bridge the gap between the information from market research and the company's internal data sources. Data Matching involves the bringing together of (typically) transactional information and attitudinal knowledge to provide a more holistic picture about the customer base than can be gained by looking at these sets of information individually. This process can greatly enhance the ability of an organization to be customer centric.

Chart no. 2

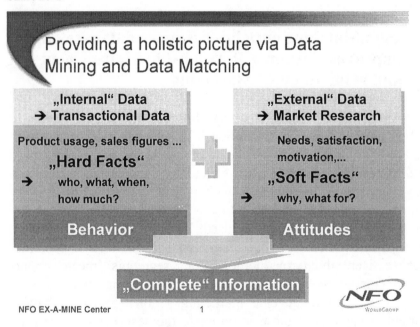

In essence Data Matching enables knowledge and information gathered from a sample of customers to be retrospectively applied to a complete customer database. In the same manner it allows newly attracted customers to be classified using the same criteria.

The opportunity is to benefit from this latent information potential in terms of:

1. Building a comprehensive customer segmentation.

2. Developing fine tuned propositions and marketing strategies which more effectively target and communicate to specific segments with, e.g., highest purchase/usage probability, (or potential), and the highest profitability.

3. Maximize customer acquisition and reduce churn, especially of profitable customer groups.

4. Increase Customer Lifetime Values and overall sales and profitability by means of cross- and up selling.

The general aim of Data Matching is to make marketing communications more effective (at a one-to-one or one-to-segment level) in generating sales. These benefits will actually be realized by focusing activity upon homogeneous groups, where individuals within the groups display the same or similar characteristics. This will result in more efficient target orientated activity, which will enhance the effectiveness of a company's CRM strategy.

For example:

- Targeting homogenous segments will lead to cost benefits due to higher response rates in mailings etc.

- Re-selling/Cross-selling/Up-selling opportunities will be able to be identified and exploited.

- Churn risk will be able to be established per segment and action taken to prevent the churn of profitable customers, before it is too late to act.

- The Customer Lifetime Value (CLV) will be boosted – both by maximizing investment in profitable customers and minimizing effort amongst low value/unprofitable customers.

"Why do we have to undertake Data Matching and why can the results from the market research study of my clients not be directly applied to the customer base?" These are questions we are frequently asked by our clients and which we will answer in the following section.

There are various reasons why results from market research have to be kept anonymous. First of all, market research companies have to follow specific privacy protection guidelines (as well as conventions by ESOMAR and national marketing associations) and would need the informed consent of the interviewees in order to use the personalized results. This could however lead to a severe bias in the answering behavior. When the clients know that their answers will be directly linked to their customer records, they will anticipate the potential consequences of their replies and modify them accordingly instead of expressing their real opinion. From the companies' point of view in most cases they want to interview only a sample of their customers because interviewing everybody would be too expensive and time consuming. Afterwards however, the insights gained with this sample of clients will be applied to the whole customer database and for these clients only the internal information is available. So a Data Matching model has to be built to transfer the information from the interviews to the customer database.

The process of Data Matching is of course dependent on there being a number of comparable measures – called "link" variables – between the customer database and the survey data being matched to it. Once these links have been established it is then possible to project estimates of attitudinal and behavioral information between the data sets.

There are two ways to ensure that sufficient potential links exist between the current segmentation study and the client's database:

1. If the survey is based on a sample of clients, all the information available in the company's databases about their customers can be used.

2. If the survey is based on a (representative) sample of the population, link variables have to be included within the questionnaire which match the fields on the company's customer database. These questions could include:

- Age of account holder
- Postcode
- Household composition
- Lifestyle
- Transactions
- ...

It should be noted, however, that answers regarding past behavior are rather error-prone. The strategy mentioned above, to use the already available database contents directly, is thus the clear first choice.

The two ways provide us with the framework to look for synergistic links between the survey data and the database, using the EX▪A▪MINE suite of Data Matching algorithms. The technical details of the Data Matching process are described in the appendix.

Where there is sufficient synergy across the link variables it will be possible to append the probability that each entry in the database has of belonging to each of the four TRI*M types. An estimated TRI*M Index can therefore be added for each customer in the database. According to this information, appropriate marketing action can then be taken as necessary. By applying this technique to the whole of the database, a complete picture of transactional and attitudinal information can be built.

It should be noted that the process of Data Matching is driven by marketing concepts rather than by statistical skills alone. The NFO EX▪A▪MINE Center works in close conjunction with the NFO market companies and our client's marketing team to ensure that the

94

analysis provides the most actionable information relevant to the company's current and future potential position.

7.4 Application: Case Study "Vaillant Excellence Process"

In this section we illustrate the process of Data Matching by a practical application which was implemented at Vaillant, the leading European producer of systems for residential warmth and water heating.

Vaillant has always been putting a strong focus on the ongoing improvement of its processes and client handling by putting market research results into direct action. The strong interaction between market research and the operative process owner of Vaillant, in which's center the PSP (=Process for Solving Problems) stands, supports the finding of an actionable and valuable solution. In the figure below it can be seen at which stages of the PSP TRI*M and EX∎A∎MINE enter the game.

Chart no. 3

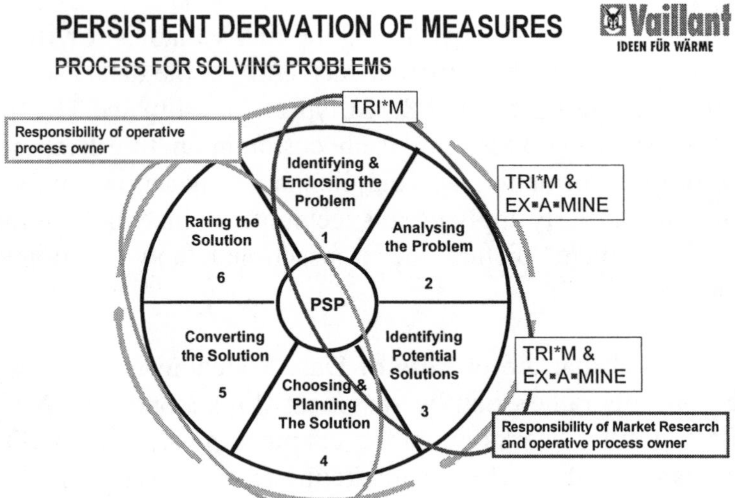

PERSISTENT DERIVATION OF MEASURES   Vaillant
IDEEN FÜR WÄRME

PROCESS FOR SOLVING PROBLEMS

The Global NFO TRI*M Center has been conducting international customer satisfaction studies for Vaillant since 1992. In 2000 the NFO EX▪A▪MINE Center carried out a Data Matching project for Vaillant in order to enrich the marketing database of Vaillant with information from a TRI*M Tracking survey. This survey had been conducted in Germany in three different business areas of Vaillant. The EX▪A▪MINE project focused on Heating Systems, the most important business area of Vaillant. Only survey data from 1999 (more than 1.000 respondents) was considered for the Data Matching in order to ensure a common time reference with the marketing database of Vaillant. The aim of the EX▪A▪MINE project was to build a model that allowed the matching of TRI*M Customer Types to the marketing database of Vaillant on a customer level. The TRI*M Customer Types express the customers' satisfaction and loyalty.

In the **first step** the NFO EX▪A▪MINE Center and Vaillant discussed prospects considering behavioral and attitudinal information within the 'Excellence Process' of Vaillant and how decisive measures for customer care could be derived by combining them.

The **second step** encompassed the understanding and collection of different data sources that were available for the Data Matching.

Vaillant had handed over the addresses on which the survey sample was based on (with the unique database key) to NFO Infratest. These addresses were over sampled, meaning that there were more addresses included in the address file than people who were actually been interviewed. At NFO for each interviewee only the database key and the respective interview number were stored. Since the addresses had been deleted the survey data was absolutely anonymous.

The link between the interview number and the customer key of the marketing database at NFO permitted the NFO EX▪A▪MINE Center to merge information from the marketing database of Vaillant with the customer types of the TRI*M Tracking survey. The database information from Vaillant was handed over on an anonymous level, hence the combined data was also anonymous.

One of the most important steps for the success of the Data Matching project was to discover the relevant information in the marketing database. The performance of the Data Matching model decisively relies on the quality of the input data. Therefore the NFO EX▪A▪MINE Center worked in close cooperation with Vaillant in revealing potentially important database fields for the Data Matching problem. Information about transactions and campaigns are collected in the marketing database of Vaillant, thus it was necessary to assign these occurrences to single customers and to transform and aggregate different fields from a relational database system to one flat file on a customer level. Finally we merged the database extraction ("hard facts") with the TRI*M customer types ("soft facts") from the TRI*M Tracking survey data to one analysis file on a customer level. On this file we based our further investigations.

In **step three** we prepared the data in order to facilitate the later applied algorithms discovering patterns. The data preparation comprises:

– Data quality checks.
– Handling of missing values.
– Handling of outliers.
– Transformation of categorical data.
– Relation of different variables to each other (for example, turnover per employee).

It is very important to consult the database responsible at the client's side, especially in order to clarify possible causes for missing values or emerging outliers. Missing values for example can have these different causes:

– The field (e.g. turnover in a certain product category) for the customer was not updated.

- The customer's volume of sales in this category is zero.

- The customer is not eligible for this product category (the volume of sales is neither zero nor equal to any other finite number).

The imputation of missing values would be different in each of these three cases.

Having prepared the data we were able to launch **step four**, the modeling part. We evaluated different algorithms in order to find the best rules for the prediction of the TRI*M customer type on an individual customer level. Since there is no single algorithm which dominates all other algorithms under various conditions (e.g. number of variables, underlying true function, model deployment, …), the NFO EX▪A▪MINE Center always applies a comprehensive toolbox consisting of algorithms from Multivariate Statistics, Machine Learning Schemes and Neural Networks. In this project the best performing model was a neural network (Cascade Correlation Learning Architecture) with an accuracy of almost 72%.

Now the Data Matching model was applied to the customer database. This is possible, because the rules refer to variables that are stored in the database of Vaillant (link variables). Applying the Data Matching model is not handing over the survey results, because there is no delivery of the personalized survey data to the client! For each customer in the database, only the predicted customer type and the predicted probability of belonging to this customer type (or the rules for the assignment) were handed over to Vaillant.

In order to evaluate the usefulness of the Data Matching model for Vaillant, the TRI*M Customer Types were explained to their sales force. Then each sales representative was asked to classify his customers according to the TRI*M types. Afterwards the sales force's estimated classification was compared to the classification of the Data Matching model. This revealed that the degree of matching between the two classifications was directly related to the degree of success of the individual sales representative: the better the match, the higher the profit generated by the respective sales representative. The sales representatives were enthusiastic about the classification model and thought it to be highly useful for their work, especially for inexperienced sales representatives.

The identification of segments now allows Vaillant to adapt their marketing activities in a better way to the specific needs of each of the segments: The "needs segments" are an operative base for the account managers and sales staff for effective communication and information of their respective clients. Not only the marketing activities are now better tailored to the individual customer, but also the spending of the marketing budget and the sales approach are optimized.

The classification system is not static: As in any modeling and estimation process, individual clients might be misclassified, and the direct contact with the client reveals this. Thus, a possibility for "manual correction" of the model by the sales force is provided and any valuable personal experience further enhances the database and helps it to be up-to-date. This "correction mode" also enables the monitoring of the Data Matching model: When the need for corrections becomes too frequent, there is a good chance that the model is out-dated and will have to be replaced.

At Vaillant the combination of TRI*M and EX■A■MINE has laid the base for a truly working customer relationship management system. Other successful applications of TRI*M and EX■A■MINE include major companies from the financial services industry, telecommunications, automotive and consumer goods.

Literature

Fayad, U., Piatetsky-Shapiro, G., Smyth, P., Uthurusamy, R. (1996): *Advances in Knowledge Discovery and Data Mining*. AAAI Press, MIT Press, Cambridge, Massachusetts, USA

Pyle, D. (1999): *Data Preparation for Data Mining*. Morgan Kaufmann Publishers, Inc. San Francisco, CA

Witten, H., Frank, E. (2000): *Data Mining – practical machine learning tools and techniques with JAVA implementations*. Morgan Kaufmann Publishers, Inc. San Francisco, CA

Appendix

Data Matching – Technical Details

In the following, the two basic means of Data Matching mentioned above will be explained in more detail.

1. If the survey is based on a sample of clients, the process of the Data Matching is the following:

   a. Our client hands the addresses of his customers on which the survey shall be based over to NFO Infratest. These addresses are over sampled, meaning that there are more addresses included in the address file than people who will actually be interviewed. The address files which are sent to NFO Infratest contain only the addresses and the unique account number for each client, but no further information about the customers. A unique identifier has to be contained in the address file so that the transactional information can be appended to the survey data as explained in the later steps. All transactional data, socio-demographic information and the other variables about the client which are stored in the company internal databases are removed from this file. Now the survey is performed. The survey data itself is anonymous, it contains a unique key of each respondent which is assigned by NFO Infratest. The link between the unique NFO-key and the respective account number are stored in a separate file which allows us to merge data from the customer database with the survey data later on. The contents of the client's customer database are screened. In this step it has to be decided, what the potentially explaining criteria with respect to the target of the Data Matching model (TRI*M loyalty types) are and which of these variables shall be appended to the survey data.

   b. The potentially selective link variables are sent to NFO Infratest with the customer-ID, but without any personal information appended (like names, addresses, etc.). As

NFO has no link in its data between the customer-ID and the name, address etc. of the "real person", the information is thus anonymous for NFO.

e. Now the link variables are merged with the survey data via the account number.

f. Having constructed one dataset containing the survey information ("soft facts") and the data from the customer database ("hard facts"), the Data Matching model is built. For the building of the model, Data Mining algorithms are applied which lead to segment specific rules, like the following:

"IF product usage = tariff 1

AND usage volume > $xx

THEN share of apostles = 78%"

g. Now the Data Matching model is applied to the customer database:

"IF product usage = tariff 1

AND usage volume > $xx

THEN probability of apostles = 78%".

We can see here, that there is a shift from the share of apostles in the sample to the probability of being an apostle in the customer database. This shift is justified by the principle of "inference by analogy". With the people interviewed being a representative sample of the entire database, it can be assumed, that the subpopulation exhibits the same behavior and patterns as the entire population and thus the statistical inference from a part to the whole is legitimate.

It is clear that applying the Data Matching model is not handing over the survey results, because there is no delivery of the personalized survey data to the client!

Chart no. 4

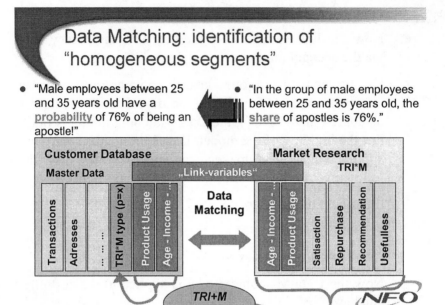

Data Matching: identification of "homogeneous segments"

- "Male employees between 25 and 35 years old have a probability of 76% of being an apostle!"

- "In the group of male employees between 25 and 35 years old, the share of apostles is 76%."

Customer Database | **Market Research** TRI*M

Master Data | „Link-variables"

Transactions | Adresses | ... ... | TRI*M type (p=x) | Product Usage | Age - Income - ... | **Data Matching** | Age - Income - ... | Product Usage | Satisaction | Repurchase | Recommendation | Usefulless

NFO EX-A-MINE Center 5/2001

TRI+M type

NFO WORLDGROUP

2. If the survey is based on a representative sample of the population, the approach is slightly different. In this case there is no possibility to merge link variables from the customer database to the survey data via a common key in order to build the Data Matching model. Thus the potentially selective link variables that are present in the customer database have to be explicitly asked in the survey. This leads to the following steps:

   a. First, the client's customer database has to be screened: What are the potentially selective and explaining criteria for the matching target (TRI*M loyalty types)?

   b. Then these link variables are included in the questionnaire, paying special attention to potential error-sources arising when asking interviewees for past product usage and purchase behavior.

c. Now the survey is conducted using the "enriched" questionnaire.

d. The Data Matching model is built using a dataset containing the survey data and the link variables, which "emulate" the contents of the customer database.

e. The Data Matching model is applied to the customer database.

8 Company-specific deployment of TRI*M results

Hans-Jochen Brückner

8.1 The Vaillant Company

Vaillant was founded in 1874 and has developed into Europe's leading supplier of heating appliances. In 2001, the workforce of 7,500 achieved a turnover of €1.3 billion, of which more than 70% was earned abroad. The introduction of Vaillant Excellence based on the EFQM (European Foundation of Quality Management) model has led to all the business processes at Vaillant being set out in detail and customer satisfaction being given the highest priority in all processes.

Chart no. 1

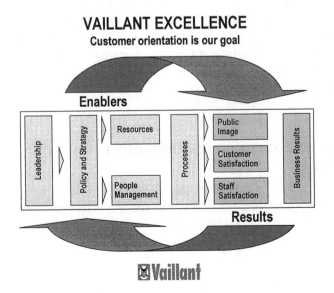

VAILLANT EXCELLENCE
Customer orientation is our goal

Chart no. 2

INTEGRATION INTO THE
BUSINESS PROCESSES

Vaillant Excellence

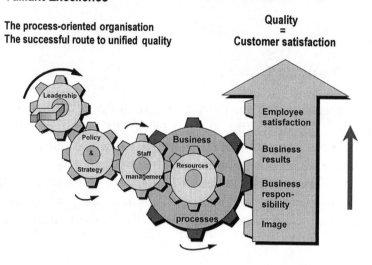

Customer satisfaction as a goal is defined within the context of the Excellence model as follows: customers are so satisfied that they will always recommend and buy Vaillant products and prefer Vaillant as the supplier of their choice. The company's success with process-orientation is apparent in the fact that in 1999, Vaillant was a finalist for the EQA (European Quality Award) and was therefore the best company in the heating sector; it also won the Ludwig Erhardt German quality prize in 1999.

8.2 Customer Retention as Vaillant's primary objective

To achieve customer retention, several success factors need to be addressed:

- Accepted measurement

- Deriving of measures

- Liability of measures

Success factor No. 1: Accepted measurement

Application of the TRI*M method since the beginning of the 1990s has brought Vaillant great advantages. The philosophy of TRI*M (Measuring, Managing, Monitoring) also superbly fits into the Vaillant Excellence process. For instance, in the year 2000 within the context of a TRI*M program about 1000 specialist technicians (installers) in Germany and 1400 technicians in 14 European sales markets were questioned by Vaillant. The tool itself and the relevant results have been adopted by senior management and other relevant levels. The method (using grids) has been accepted and learned. In my view, this is a precondition for the consistent deriving and implementing of measures.

Success factor No. 2: Deriving of Measures

Within the context of the Excellence model, there are two tools available to Vaillant for the deriving of appropriate measures: QIP (the Quality Improvement Process) and PSP (the Problem Solving Process). The process of measure derivation will now be explained using the example of PSP:

Chart no. 3:

THE PROBLEM SOLVING PROCESS (PSP)

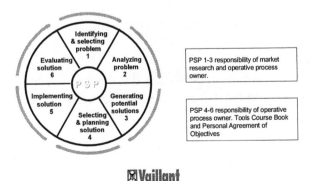

Vaillant

PSP Step 1: Identifying and selecting the problem

The result of the TRI*M questionnaire represents in each country - and also in Germany - a snapshot of current customer satisfaction and customer loyalty in relation to a selected product or service feature. In the first step, a problem statement is set out in terms of the gap between the "actual" and "desired" states.

PSP Step 2: Analyzing the problem

In this step, within the setting of a workshop with the affected managers from the Vaillant organization, the main reasons for the "actual" evaluation in Step 1 are worked out using, for instance, an Ishikawa diagram. Discussion of problems and challenges is decisive for uniform understanding of the problem and the deriving of relevant measures.

PSP Step 3: Generating potential solutions

In this step, a gathering together of possible solutions to the problems identified in Steps 1 and 2 is undertaken. This is done by means, for instance, of brainstorming or a metaplan technique.

Steps 1-3 of the PSP are jointly carried out by the Market Research department and the operative process owners in the Vaillant organizations.

PSP Step 4: Selecting and planning solutions

In this step, measures are prioritized and selected. Selection criteria for measures may be the resource deployment or the "moment of truth" (the speed at which the customer notices a change).

PSP Step 5: Implementing solutions

In this step, the measures are adapted to the standard processes. As in Step 4, the operative process owner again is responsible.

PSP Step 6: Evaluating solutions

Whether the implemented solution/measure has the desired success with the customer is tested both by the operative process owner and in the context of further market research studies.

In the interest of increasing customer satisfaction and customer loyalty, it is necessary that the improvement processes should be binding on the individual employee. And in order to ensure this bindingness, in the context of the Excellence process, "course books" defining the measures decided upon in the field of customer satisfaction and setting out target values are written for every Vaillant organizational unit. From these course books for every organizational unit, employee target agreements are derived, so that in every target agreement, the measures for enhancing customer satisfaction are shown in cascaded arrangement.

In order to increase the operational deployment of TRI*M results in this context, "item bundles" have been defined.

In a first step, the responsibility of an operative or strategic process owner is agreed for the relevant item bundle. The item bundle owners are primarily recruited from the top management. For every item bundle, three values are calculated, which are then entered into the goal agreements for the leadership.

8.3 Monitoring of strategic goals with bundle indicator values

1st step: Bundling of TRI*M performance elements
The TRI*M performance elements are grouped together based on the information from the TRI*M grid to form "item bundles". A *connection in terms of content* between the elements is essential. In addition, the following aspects are taken into account for the bundling process:

- similar positioning in the TRI*M grid,

- similar current customer assessment,

- interdependencies between the individual elements.

For every bundle, two indicator values based on customer satisfaction surveys can be calculated: performance and impact.

Performance

Every responsible individual knows whether his area is assessed as being good or bad and how it compares with the TRI*M Index value of the company.

Impact

It is the aim of TRI*M to focus on investment. The measure called impact shows where the greatest lever effect is achieved.

Based on this information, target values can be laid out for various different periods. For the setting of targets, it is first necessary to formulate achievable and sensible target values.

2nd step: Performance evaluation for each item bundle

For each item bundle - comprising individual TRI*M performance elements - an average performance symbol is calculated taking into account the significance of each individual quality element. The average bundle performance is reflected in the TRI*M Index of the whole company.

An average bundle corresponds to the TRI*M Index of the company. A well-assessed bundle achieves a higher index value, while a poorly assessed bundle achieves a lower index value. Every person responsible for a bundle knows where he/she stands. Major improvements do not depend only on the improvement of the person's own bundle, but also on the development of the overall index. Gaining the advantage at the expense of others is futile.

3rd step: Impact

The impact of an item bundle is dependent on the grid position of the bundle elements:

- The diagonal of the TRI*M grid from the lower left corner of the "potential/?" sector to the upper right corner of the "Motivators" sector extends from 0 to 10.

- The diagonal from the upper left corner of the "Hygienics" sector to the bottom right corner of the "Hidden Opportunities" sector runs from 3 to 7, since the significance of communication to action corresponds to a ratio of 3 to 7.

The impact of each bundle is known. Actions may be concentrated on the bundle with the greatest impact.

4th step: Determination of target values

When setting concrete target parameters, situational and strategic viewpoints are taken into account.

- Determination of the improvement opportunities for the individual bundle (how simple is it to achieve a higher value?).

- Preparation of the decision as to which bundles to invest in (what value do we wish to achieve?).

- Determination of the influence of a bundle usable in the planning period (how necessary is it to achieve a high value?).

For each bundle it is determined how simple the assessment of the bundle can be improved. Measurement of the number of moments of truth and thereby determination of the speed with which the customers notice a change:

I   - Changes are perceived by customers after a delay.

II   - Changes are perceived by customers at short notice.

For every bundle, target values are set, taking into account the intended investment and with consideration of the sequential curves.

Investment and target values are stipulated for every responsible person based on the influence of the various bundles This can be used optimally in the planning period for enhancing customer loyalty.

The combination of measured variables for the relevant item bundles ensures that the company concentrates on the right items bundles - that is, those of particular relevance to customers - and can thereby specifically deploy its resources for enhancing customer satisfaction and customer loyalty. In addition, based upon the curve shapes, target values are defined which, depending upon the available resources, are realistic and acceptable to the item bundle owners. The target values agreed with the senior management or the relevant superior for each item bundle are coupled to an extra premium. This means that achievement of the target values in the year 2001 results in the special premium of "customer satisfaction and customer loyalty" for the item bundle owner. The logic of Vaillant Excellence in view of the cascading of aims for each organizational unit and of the top management has the result that the target values are also reflected, broken down into detailed targets, in the target agreements of the individual employee.

9 The Customer Retention Index as a marketing performance measurement tool for trade fairs

Alex Ulrich

9.1 Introduction

Exhibitions are market events at which the market participants meet each other over the course of a few days at an exhibition center. For both sides - suppliers and buyers or exhibitors and visitors - taking part in a trade fair is a multi-functional marketing instrument in the selling or purchasing process.

The structure of the exhibition industry in Germany has a peculiarity in that the exhibition companies are not only organizers of the events they hold, but also owners and operators of the exhibition centers themselves.

Chart no. 1

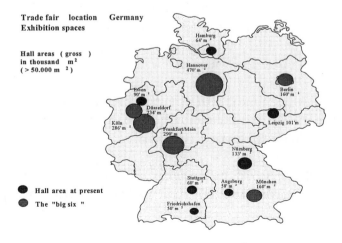

Trade fair location Germany
Exhibition spaces

Hall areas (gross)
in thousand m^2
(> 50.000 m^2)

● Hall area at present
● The "big six "

Hamburg 64' m^2
Hannover 470' m^2
Essen 90' m^2
Berlin 160' m^2
Düsseldorf 234' m^2
Köln 286' m^2
Frankfurt/Main 290' m^2
Leipzig 101'm^2
Nürnberg 133' m^2
Stuttgart 60' m^2
Augsburg 58' m^2
München 160' m^2
Friedrichshafen 50' m^2

Messe München GmbH (MMG) is one of the six largest exhibition organizers in Germany, alongside Hanover, Frankfurt, Cologne, Düsseldorf and Berlin.

Like almost all of the German exhibition companies, it is owned by public bodies, specifically mainly the city of Munich and the state of Bavaria.

Chart no. 2

The New Munich Trade Fair Centre

- Shareholders: City of Munich 49.9%, Free State of Bavaria 49.9%, Chamber of Industry and Commerce for Munich and Upper Bavaria 0.2%
- Purpose: Securing and expanding the position of Munich as a trade fair location
- Number of employees: approximately 450 (MMG parent company)
- Turnover: approximately DM 350 - 400 million
- Hall area at trade fair grounds: 280,000 sqm on open-air sites

    160,000 sqm in halls

The role of Messe München consists in securing and developing the position of Munich as a location for exhibitions and trade fairs. Profit is not the main motive, but it is the intention that Messe München should at least cover its own costs.

MMG's products are its exhibitions, of which it puts on about 30 each year, most of them on an international scale, although some have a more national or regional focus.

As customers the company serves more than 30,000 exhibitors from over 90 countries and at least 2 million visitors from at least 150 countries each year.

9.2 Customer surveys

MMG gathers information about its customers from exhibition questionnaires, which it carries out during exhibitions. The exhibitor questionnaire takes the form of a written full-scale survey involving all the exhibitor stands. Among visitors, a representative sample of at least 500 - 2000 persons is questioned during the exhibition in a computer-assisted questionnaire. These surveys bring advantages, above all, in the areas of marketing, PR and statistics.

Chart no. 3

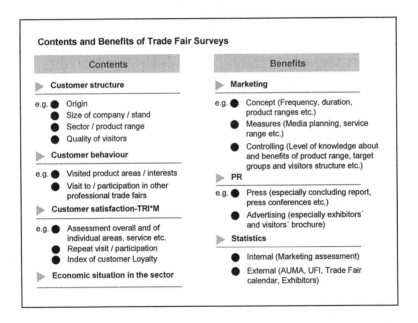

Apart from determining the clientele structure (e.g. origin and quality of the visitors, exhibitors' stand size), customer behavior (e.g. media behavior, visits to or participation at other specialist exhibitions), assessment of the economic situation, etc., measurement of customer satisfaction and customer loyalty is a central component of exhibition surveys. This is where the TRI*M Index comes into use.

Chart no. 4 offers an overview of the TRI*M Index for exhibitions and customer groups, i.e. for exhibitors and visitors at an exhibition.

Chart no. 4

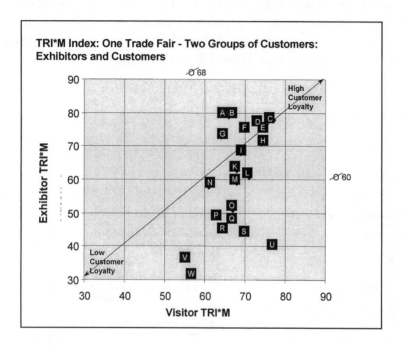

Since the exhibitors have a higher level of involvement in an exhibition than the visitors - particularly through greater financial commitment - the TRI*M Index varies more strongly here. It extends from 30 to more than 80 points, with an average value of about 68 points. As is shown by the exhibition at "U", for instance, a higher index value on the visitor side does not always correspond to a higher index on the exhibitor side and vice versa. As an average tendency, however, the TRI*M indices of both customer groups move in the same direction.

A high or low TRI*M Index on the exhibitor or visitor side correlates strongly with the main performance elements of the exhibition from the viewpoint of the exhibitor or visitor. The main performance elements for assessment that are addressed here and in all exhibition surveys have been found in earlier surveys to be the elements that have a large influence on customer loyalty and are therefore more than just hygienics. The high individual valuation of factors such as visitor frequency, internationality of the visitors, quality of the visitors, leading exhibition character (= market leadership), exhibitor service and clarity by exhibitors lead to a high level of satisfaction and a high TRI*M Index on the part of exhibitors, and vice versa.

An Average Trade Fair Year in Figures:
Approximately 30 international trade fairs and
approximately 280 guest events:

- More than 30,000 exhibitors from more than 90 countries.
- More than two million visitors from more than 150 countries.

The larger the spread in the assessment of an individual performance element between an exhibition with a high TRI*M Index (Exhibition 1) and exhibition with a very low index value (Exhibition 2), the greater is the influence of this statement on the TRI*M Index. Here, the exhibitor service has hardly any influence on the exhibitor index, since although it was similarly assessed at the two exhibitions, the index value for the two exhibitions was fundamentally different.

In addition, at certain exhibitions, parallels can be identified between the individual assessments of exhibitors and visitors. If, for instance, the exhibitors ascribe a leading exhibition character to a particular exhibition, the corresponding assessment on the visitors' side often also comes out positive.

Alongside the correlation of the TRI*M Index with the individual performance elements also the relationship between the development of exhibitor and visitor indices and the development of exhibition occupancy (measured by the area rented by the exhibitors) over time for a particular exhibition is worth mentioning.

118

With rising or falling occupancy at an exhibition, the trend in the exhibitor and visitor indices also tends to rise or fall. A larger number of exhibitors and the associated greater choice for visitors (as one of the main performance elements) generally results in greater satisfaction and numbers of visitors (visitor frequency). This also provides for greater satisfaction levels among the exhibitors.

So how valid is the TRI*M Index and how does the measured customer loyalty and repeat participation intention of exhibitors relate to actual repeat participation at the next exhibition?
Exhibitions are sorted according to likelihood of repeat participation and according to the number of respondents who "definitely" intend to participate at the next exhibition.

Chart no. 5

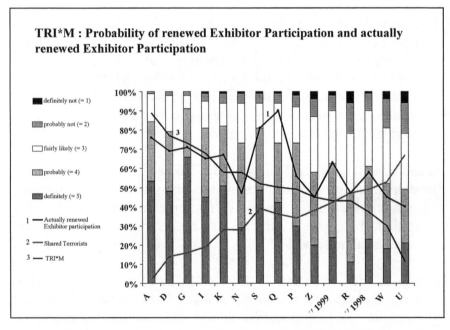

The stacked bars show the result of the question about intention towards repeat participation at the next exhibition. The continuous line marks the actual repeat participation quota. The result confirms that the intention expressed at the exhibition and actual behavior in future agree very well. The actual repeat participation quota is usually given by the sum of the proportions of respondents who will "certainly" or "probably" exhibit at the next event. It may, however, lie below this sum if, for instance, the fluctuation of businesses in the sector is very large, as is the case with exhibitions that are held only once every few years. This relatively precise prediction arises from the fact that at the exhibition only those persons are asked who are qualified for such a survey by virtue of their position in the company. The TRI*M Index is therefore valid and has predictive power.

This leads to use of the TRI*M Index as an early warning indicator.

Chart no. 6

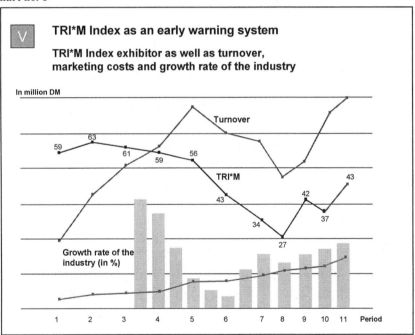

The study period here extends over a relatively long timeframe (11 periods). Customer loyalty - also measured with the TRI*M Index - is shown by the blue line. Demand among customers - that is the renting of stand space by the exhibitors and the number of exhibitors - substantially determine the turnover of an exhibition event (the red line). An environmental factor that cannot be influenced by the exhibition company, the development of the industry, is measured here by its growth rate (the green bar). The activities of the exhibition company are reflected in the marketing costs (Marcom, purple line).

Customer satisfaction and loyalty - i.e. the TRI*M Index - falls from period 2 onward, while the turnover continues to rise because the industry is booming and new customers are being acquired. Only when the boom tails off, does the falling customer loyalty make its effect felt on turnover. Marketing expenditure has probably been increased too late and too little. The result is a downward spiral. With increased marketing expenditure and the industry upturn to help it, customer satisfaction and turnover rise again strongly from period 9 onwards.

Another possibility for representing the correlation between customer perspective and financial perspective is shown by chart no. 6.

These two perspectives of the Balanced Scorecard are represented here as a portfolio. Customer loyalty has been measured using the TRI*M Index of the exhibitors, since the largest part of turnover comes from them. The efficiency of an exhibition, as far as the financial perspective is concerned, is measured using the gross yield quota (marginal income quota). On average, one can see a positive correlation between customer loyalty and financial efficiency (profitability).

For Messe München, therefore, the TRI*M Index has become the main financial indicator of the customer perspective on the Balanced Scorecard.

This also provides a helpful picture for use in internal bench-marking. Also to be considered, however, is the stage at which an exhibition takes place: if it is new and there is a need to invest in customer satisfaction, the financial yield may be small or negative (exhibition A). Later, when the exhibition is established, it brings in a lot of money, but requires relatively less marketing expenditure given a greater level of customer loyalty, the gross yield quota is high. The positive correlation between customer loyalty and financial efficiency becomes still clearer if the two exhibitions A and E are excluded. Both are exhibitions that have been held less than three times. If A and E are left out, the S-curve can be more exactly fitted to the point distribution.

Chart no. 7

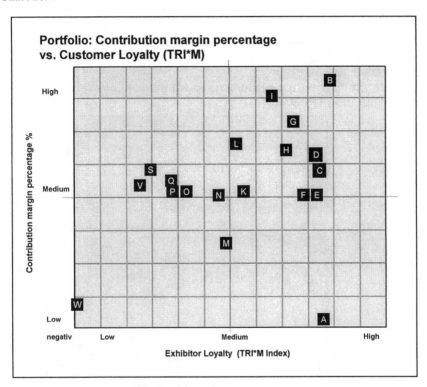

The link between customer loyalty and marketing expenditure is still clearer in chart no. 7.

Here, the expenditure for Marcom as % of turnover is becoming ever smaller the greater the customer loyalty (the TRI*M Index) becomes.

122

Only exhibition A as a new product, in which further investment is needed despite a high index value, does not fit the pattern.

This chart shows very clearly:

- Customer satisfaction costs money.

- Customer loyalty brings money.

Chart no. 8

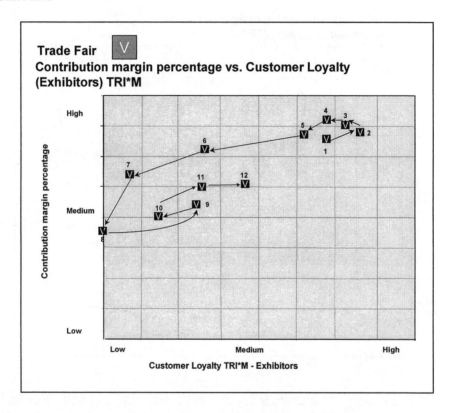

Chart no. 8 shows this relationship as a chronological sequence using the example of exhibition V, which was previously shown in by using a practical example chart no. 6. If customer loyalty - the TRI*M Index - falls, then sooner or later profitability - the gross yield quota of the exhibition - also falls.

Since there is always a certain time delay, this relationship is not represented by a sloping straight line, but rather as a circle or a flat ellipse over the 11 periods shown here.

Summarizing, it can be said that customer loyalty measurement with the aid of an index offers excellent possibilities for marketing assessment. Even in a highly specialized service sector like the exhibition industry, the TRI*M system proves to be a very useful tool.

10 Auditing firms today and tomorrow

Dr. Joachim Scharioth, Norma van den Berk

NFO Infratest

The following article demonstrates how NFO TRI*M can be used not only for analysis in the present, but also to draw out the expectations and concerns of customers in relation to the future.

10.1 Aims and design of the investigation

Auditing firms are facing new challenges today, the like of which hardly any other group has to reckon with. Their range of services now extends from traditional auditing to consultancy services and the highly topical area of risk management.

Against this background, NFO Infratest was commissioned by the top 500 businesses in Germany - i.e. by their most important customers - to conduct an assessment of the largest auditing firms. The study also concerned itself with the question, from the viewpoint of the largest companies, of how well the auditing firms have prepared themselves for the challenges of the future.

The results show how this sector needs to orient and position itself to fulfill the expectations of its clients not only today, but also in the future.

In all, 72 leaders within the largest companies in Germany were questioned over the telephone. 1/5 of the businesses involved buy only the firms' statutory auditing services, while 4/5 of them make use of their extensive consultancy services.

In addition to their positions of leadership in their own company, 2 out of every 5 of those questioned were also active on the supervisory boards of other companies.

Chart no. 1

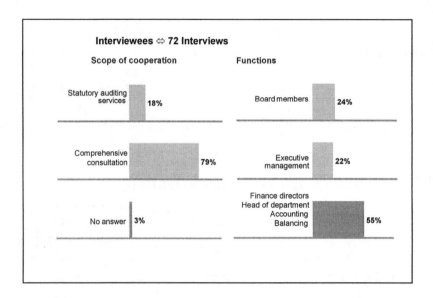

10.2 The most important results

In the customers' views, competition between the auditing firms is becoming more intense, since customers feel freer in their choice of auditor and in moving from one to another.

The client companies want their auditors to be a partner who accompanies them through the ever-growing challenges of planning and reporting their financial management. Consultancy or support reaching beyond this service is of secondary importance.

To this end, customers would like a more transparent, but tighter organization in the auditing firms than is the case today. They place a high value on a competent consultant empowered to take decisions who thinks entrepreneurially, is proactive and independent, but whose formal position plays no part. This consultant constitutes the decisive factor in the success or failure of an auditing firm and of the customer-orientation that is of ever growing importance to this business.

Chart no. 2

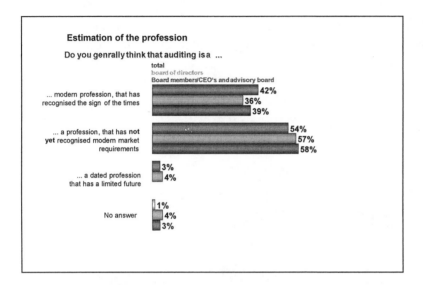

Clients regard the auditing firms as lacking in innovation and being unprepared or inadequately prepared for the challenges of the future.

More than half of those questioned see auditing as a profession that has not yet recognized the demands of the market. Only 2 out of 5 respondents and only one in every 3 supervisory board members were of the opinion that auditors as a group perceive the signs of the times. There is a necessity for auditing firms to communicate better internally as well as externally about their preparation for the demands of tomorrow. They must concentrate much more effort on marketing in the future if they are to dispel this negative image among their customers about their activities.

10.3 Customer loyalty

The strength of customer loyalty to the auditing firms is assessed as average. On a scale with a maximum value of 100 and on which values below 40 signal-disappointed customers, auditing firms achieve an index value of 66.

By comparison, the value for services in the B2B sector in Germany is about the same and stands at 63. If the level of preparation for the challenges of the next 5 years is examined, the value for the auditors falls as low as 56.

Chart no. 3

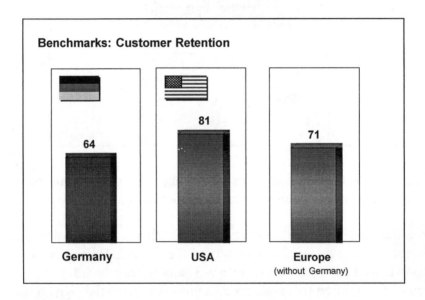

Companies that make use of comprehensive consultancy services from auditing companies assess them markedly better than those who buy only the minimum service. The value of the services provided is estimated significantly higher, although the assessment with regard to preparation for the future comes out 10 points lower.

Chart no. 4

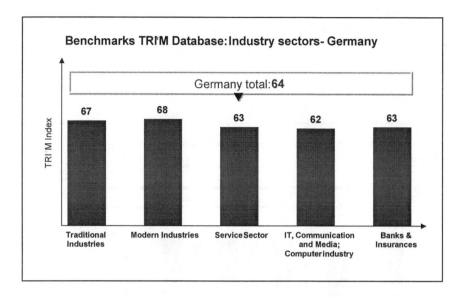

Auditing firms are rated most highly by the 2nd or 3rd hierarchy levels. Directors and supervisory board members evaluate their customer loyalty levels much lower. And given that auditors should primarily enable management and supervisory boards to keep control, this outcome is not entirely unproblematic. With regard to the preparation of auditing firms for future challenges, the survey respondents are largely unanimous.

In order to measure customer loyalty levels, the NFO TRI*M Index was used. This is an instrument used by more than 500 firms including 1/3 of the top 100 European businesses for measuring customer loyalty and which has proved itself in thousands of measurements worldwide.

The NFO TRI*M Index is based on the four Index questions which in this survey were asked in connection not only with current relations, but also regarding preparation for the future.

130

As already mentioned, the customer loyalty index value for B2B services in Germany is 64, while in Europe generally the value is 71. Interestingly, this difference exists only in the service sector (Germany still being less service-oriented), while in the manufacturing sector, there is no difference.

Chart no. 5

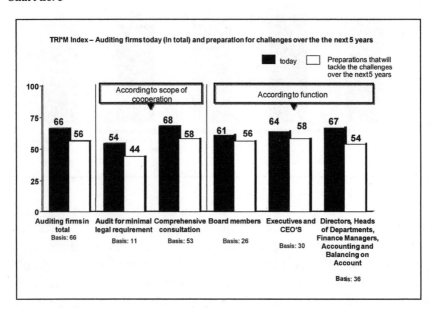

In the USA, the customer loyalty index value is significantly higher and stands at 81. This is due, above all, to the fact that in America customers are much less patient and change suppliers more readily, that means that dissatisfied customers have already changed suppliers.

For the auditing firms therefore, and for all service providers in Germany, there is a challenge to bring their sector up to the international standard as quickly as possible with regard to customer loyalty.

An analysis of the individual questions that make up the index shows that the customers have an average satisfaction level:

- 38% assess their auditors as being excellent or very good.
- 42% would recommend their auditors to others.

but only 35% ascribed a very large or large benefit for their business to the activities of the auditor firms (18% even spoke of a low or no benefit).

Nevertheless, the willingness to change auditors is low. Businesses feel tied to their auditors and definitely or probably want to continue working with the same firm in future. 61% are sure they will continue working with their existing auditors, but in their estimation of future years, the picture changes entirely. The proportion that definitely want to work with their auditing firm falls to 38%, while simultaneously a significantly greater benefit is expected.

10.4 Market resistance

Jones and Sasser, two American academics, used the variables Satisfaction and Loyalty on which they based definitions of customer types. Highly satisfied and loyal customers are known as Apostles, while their opposites are known as Terrorists. A growing segment of our society comprises Mercenaries who are highly satisfied but have the feeling that they receive the same service from different providers, and therefore place the greatest emphasis on price, which makes them disloyal. On the other side of the coin are customers who are dissatisfied, but for whom a change is virtually out of the question, because the barriers are too high for them - these are the Hostages. It is probable that Microsoft's commercial customers are currently only made up of Apostles and Hostages, because the barriers to change are too high for them. Customers may be loyal regardless of whether they are satisfied or dissatisfied.

132

Chart no. 6

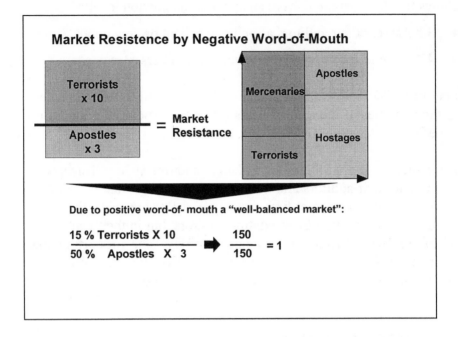

Based on this model and on the fact that, within the same period, Terrorists express significantly more negative recommendations than Apostles do positive ones, NFO Infratest has developed a market resistance value for individual businesses/providers. This value shows at a glance how high the sales expenditure is for a supplier. Suppliers who have to overcome a high market resistance must make greater investments in their sales effort than those who have a low market resistance to surmount. An average value is 1 (15% Terrorists x 10 negative recommendations divided by 50% Apostles times 3 positive recommendations).

The result of 1.25 for the auditing firms at the present time is therefore relatively good. What is particularly noticeable is the high proportion of Hostages that exists. In Germany, the average for this group in other sectors is 6%, while the proportion of Hostages with audit firms stands at 17%. What is important, however, is that in future the market resistance will drastically increase to 2.3. Above all, this is due to the growing number of Mercenaries.

Chart no. 7

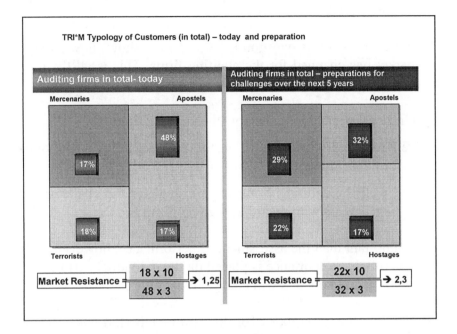

Auditing services are increasingly becoming services just like any other, and more and more often the customer buys them based on a cost/benefit ratio.

Noticeably, auditing firms will also be selected for competitive reasons. Undertaking an expansion into the consultancy business alone is not sufficient; here too, the proportion of Mercenaries will increase greatly.

Customers who already take advantage of the comprehensive services of auditing firms have a low market resistance due to their high customer loyalty. But even among them the proportion of Mercenaries will increase drastically in future and will become markedly higher than in other sectors (34% instead of about 25%).

Audit companies must think far more professionally than before, not only about their marketing, but also about their sales policy.

10.5 Performance demands of existing and potential customers

The mere fact that this question is being posed, shows how strongly the market has changed for the auditing firms. This is all the more the case, if individual performance factors are taken into account.

NFO Infratest wanted to know how the auditing firms

- are assessed by their customers regarding individual performance factors, and

- how well the auditing firms are prepared for the challenges of the next 5 years with regard to each performance factor.

More important than the assessment of performance, however, is the question of what importance is placed on the individual performance factors today and how this will change in the future.

Determining the importance of the various performance factors requires two different approaches:

- firstly, determining reported importance, i.e. what do the respondents regard as important when they are questioned.

- secondly, what performance factors influence the overall assessment of auditing firms today and tomorrow.

By bringing together "Stated Importance" and the actual impact on customer loyalty, the performance factors can be divided into 4 segments:

- Motivators - decisively important to success, since relevant on both axes.

- Hygienics – people talk about these, but the assessment of these performance factors actually has no influence on customer loyalty.

- Hidden opportunities – these factors are not yet stated as being important. In reality, they already influence customer loyalty.

- ?/Potential savings: performance factors that are not currently used for creating customer loyalty. These may develop into new hidden opportunities.

In the following, the results of the quality elements are presented in the form of a TRI*M grid. This Strength/Weakness analysis provides results on a threefold basis:

- Stated **Importance** of a service factor (vertical axis).

- **Fulfillment** of a quality element by the auditing firm in the eyes of the customers.

- The **Real Impact** of a quality factor for the assessment of the auditing company (horizontal axis).

The real impact is the only dimension that NFO Infratest does not adopt directly from the survey, but determines by using **statistical methods**.

A high real impact belongs to those performance elements with which all customers with a high index value are extremely satisfied, or for which all customers with a low index value are dissatisfied.

Therefore, there is a strong connection between the intensity of customer loyalty and the fulfillment, so that the corresponding performance factor has a high real impact on customer loyalty.

If there is no such link between index and fulfillment, then the performance factor has only a low or no real impact.

The vertical axis shows what the auditing firms communicate about, while the horizontal axis shows in what areas there is a need for action. In the case of Motivators and Hidden Opportunities that achieve no rectangle (strength), the customers see deficits in the auditing companies.

Hygienics should continue to be communicated, but there is no need for improvements. All the performance factors in the Potentials field are currently not used in the customer relationship.

Chart no. 8

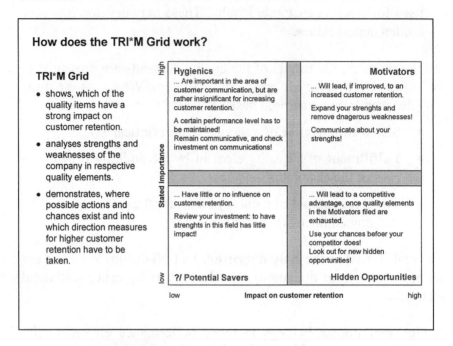

How does the TRI*M Grid work?

TRI*M Grid

- shows, which of the quality items have a strong impact on customer retention.

- analyses strengths and weaknesses of the company in respective quality elements.

- demonstrates, where possible actions and chances exist and into which direction measures for higher customer retention have to be taken.

Stated Importance (high / low)

Hygienics
... Are important in the area of customer communication, but are rather insignificant for increasing customer retention.

A certain performance level has to be maintained!
Remain communicative, and check investment on communications!

Motivators
... Will lead, if improved, to an increased customer retention.

Expand your strenghts and remove dnagerous weaknesses!

Communicate about your strengths!

?/ Potential Savers
... Have little or no influence on customer retention.

Review your investment: to have strenghts in this field has little impact!

Hidden Opportunities
... Will lead to a competitive advantage, once quality elements in the Motivators filed are exhausted.

Use your chances befoer your competitor does!
Look out for new hidden opportunities!

low — **Impact on customer retention** — high

In a grid of this type, the life cycle of individual performance factors can also be followed. It differs according to whether the individual performance factors:

- are initiated by the auditing companies,

- are required by statutory regulations.

Company-initiated performance factors start in the ?/Potential Savings field, become Hidden Opportunities, then customers see their advantage, but are not aware of their importance, they then emerge as Motivators and then, at some stage, become self-evident (Hygienics) and finally fall back again into the?/Potential Savings field.

Performance factors based on regulations follow the opposite route. First everyone says they are not relevant (Hygienics) and that they can, if they prove themselves, become Motivators.

10.5.1 The auditing firm as a business

The most important and simultaneously the most relevant factor that is well fulfilled by the auditing firms is customer orientation. It plays an absolutely decisive role in the firm's success or failure. Other strengths of the auditing firm, such as long experience, reputation with the supervisory board, internationality, wide coverage in the home market or a good international reputation and a globally unified name are now taken for granted. All these criteria are in the Hygienics segment or are very near to this segment.

Assessed as much worse or average is the innovative capability of the auditing companies and this is where a lack of marketing makes itself felt. In all these points there is no great difference between today and future requirements.

Quite a different matter is the leadership competency of the management. While today this is still assessed as being average, the companies regard the auditing firms as being well equipped to face the challenges of the next 5 years. The change to a stronger leadership competency within the auditing firms is positively assessed.

10.5.2 Organization of the auditing firm

An important motivator in this sector is the ability to draw on the experience of the head office. The range of worldwide backup services is highly estimated, although over the years it develops into a Hygiene Factor. Similarly assessed is the account principle, whereby a single contact person coordinates all the work. Customers increasingly perceive this as a self-evident standard feature.

Rotation of contact persons, on the other hand, is not appreciated by customers.

A tight organization within the context of the corporate leadership, and transparency in the auditing firm's organization are seen as

Hidden Opportunities for the future by customers. What is surprising is that the "partner structure" of the auditing firms is not regarded as a relevant advantage. The much-discussed separation of auditing and consultancy is indeed a point of interest and discussion, but plays no part in the assessment of the firms either today or for the future (it is a Hygiene factor).

The auditing firms are not succeeding in giving their customers the feeling that the best person in a particular specialization looks after the customers; nor is this really expected. It is important to customers that the contact person is competent and empowered to make decisions. However, the formal position of the contact person is not important. This is something that the auditing firms fulfill only to an average extent according to their customers.

In the customers' eyes, it is irrelevant to what extent the consultants are members of a leadership board in the firm. This opinion applies also for the needs of the future and is shared by the responding management board and supervisory board members.

10.5.3 The consultants/auditors

Although the formal position of the consultant/auditor is assessed as being unimportant, the auditors are the decisive factor in an assessment of the auditing firms. Personal and specialist competency, and their role as specialists is as highly valued as their trustworthiness, based on long years of cooperation and experience with similarly large clients, as well as the trust they enjoy within the supervisory board. These strengths are also of great significance for the future.

In addition, there are two service factors that are fulfilled only by today's consultants/auditors: the generalist profile and a strong industry-specific competency. Both become more and more important over time. Further elements in the Motivators field for which the consultants/auditors have deficits in the eyes of their customers are the business profile, their proactive behavior - i.e. own initiatives, and closely related to this, indications of business risks.

The customers also miss the support in the assessing of business prognoses, leading to a below average estimation.

NFO Infratest observes these changes in all sectors. The customer places the requirement on their service providers even more strongly that they should be proactive. Long years of good partnership requires that both partners are mutually active in order to enhance the overall level of satisfaction. The requirements placed on consultants are therefore significantly increased. Customers expect more customer orientation from their consultants, which means more identification with the customer's business.

10.5.4 The service spectrum

These changed requirements placed on consultants also find expression in expectations in relation to the range of services offered. The classical services of auditing firms,

- such as closer core services within the field of auditing (financial audit, audit report),
- support for entrepreneurial transactions (for the respective), such as, for instance, analysis of the financial indicator figures and contracts, management screening, staff potential, analysis of the market position and customer structure
- such as the range of consultancy services and
- use of uniform standards
- nationally and internationally well fulfilled Hygiene Factors

On the other hand, Hidden Opportunities that have not yet been fulfilled to the satisfaction of the customers are strategic risk management consultancy, implementation of KonTraG - i.e. the pursuit of risk-relevant indicator figures and their extension to the employee and customer structure. Brand Valuation and Value Reporting are linked to these expectations. In the future, these expectations will be enhanced by giving a greater significance to the process audit, the performance audit and consultancy for economic development of the sector and to sector comparisons and sector predictions.

Customers see a future in Internet certifications. But whether the auditing firms are ideal partners for consultancy for E-business or for IT system testing, remains an unanswered question.

In times when management is expected to make much more detailed observations of the environment, management wishes to have auditing firms standing by its side. It demands that the sector should position itself to deal with the tasks that are directly connected with business processes and business risks. To what extent additional offers will be made is not of decisive importance.

11 A memorable meeting

Rolf Hahn

11.1 Introduction

It probably occurred at one of the industry exhibitions in Hanover. As the person in charge of the Siemens stand, among other things - of greeting customers and other honored guests of the Siemens company, on one occasion, Mr. Scharioth from NFO Infratest was one of these special guests and it was a pleasure to talk and discuss with him. We rapidly alighted on a topic of great interest to both of us: quality assessment in the area of services, particularly in training. At that time I was in charge of the worldwide training activities in the field of automation for Siemens. My brief was to support the broad spectrum of new sales activities through training in such a way that Siemens would become a leading player in the automation sector. This goal was indeed achieved. In fact, in the area of core systems for automation - the stored program control systems, SPS - Siemens is now the No. 1 player in the world market. A significant precondition for this success was the transfer of an enormous amount of knowledge and experience both to the Siemens staff involved and to the staff working in this field at customer companies.

My motto in those days was: "Good training is the best advertising". However, certain hurdles stood in the way of converting this motto into monetary value and overcoming them was an exciting and essential task. And that was why I was delighted when Mr. Scharioth introduced me to TRI*M. From the time of this memorable meeting onwards, I was convinced that TRI*M represented a non-individual-dependent platform for quality assessment, and not only in the field of training.

11.2 Quality Assessment in Production and Services

On close examination, it becomes clear that there are two predominant areas for the use of quality-assurance measures: the production of goods of all kinds, and knowledge transfer.

Quality assessment in production is now a long-established field and today receives a great deal of careful attention. And no wonder, since undiscovered errors and faults often incur high remedial and replacement costs, which can rapidly bring small and medium-sized companies to the edge of financial disaster. It is an advantage - and simultaneously a characteristic - of this area of quality assurance that the current values of the key variables can be continuously monitored and tested for deviation from the target values. This can often even be achieved without interruption, without physical contact and synchronously with production. In this area of quality control, computer-controlled monitoring equipment has practically revolutionized manufacturing. Nowadays, quality assurance in production can be said to have attained a high level of perfection.

Typical of this advance, according to my observations, is the motor industry. Its products, the motor vehicles, are so reliable today one rarely sees defective cars on the hard shoulder of the motorway nowadays. A few decades ago, it was an entirely different story. Then it was through necessity that the motoring associations sent out their familiar service vehicles to keep the roads - and above all the motorways - free from broken-down vehicles.

The conclusion is that quality assessment is now seen as being an absolute necessity within the production process. Typically, graphical representations of the products to be made are drawn up by hand - or increasingly with computer-aided-design (CAD) - with details of all the nominal values and permissible tolerances.

In the service sector, the quality of services can seldom be measured objectively, and usually only subjectively assessed. In place of concrete data available for quality assessment in production, in the service sector when the people directly affected are questioned, they can offer only opinions that describe the relevant service quality more or less accurately. But here, too, the customer has the right to demand optimum performance for his or her money - a fact that is particularly true of training in automation technology. In the course participants are taught knowledge and skills that they absolutely need in order to be able to use and operate relatively complex systems in their field. Shortcomings in training almost inevitably mean poor utilization of the system characteristics, less than optimized production processes, and therefore also costs.

In the immense domain of services, however, the quality of the services rendered can seldom be objectively assessed, and frequently only subjectively. Obtaining the most objective evaluation possible is, however, an essential requirement if services are to be optimized to the benefit of the customers. NFO Infratest and I agreed upon an extremely practice-oriented case study of staff at both companies. As the object to be investigated, we chose, almost at random, some courses from the SIMATIC programme. The question to be asked was: What are the possibilities for using this type of computer-aided quality assessment in the field of training?

11.3 Different Levels of Intensity in Quality Assessment of Training

Several possibilities exist for quality assessment in the field of training. As shown in a simplified form three elementary levels can be identified:

Level 1: Assessment of satisfaction
With the aid of a questionnaire form, training participants assess various criteria with regard to their fulfillment by the provider, after which they award a grade. However, evaluation of these forms involves the following problems:

- The awarding of grades involves assessing the seminar or course, but it is frequently misunderstood as being an evaluation of the instructor.

- Immediately after conclusion of the course, the opinion of the participants is either negative or positive; from more or less bi-ased all the way through to rapturous enthusiasm. In other words, the assessment given does not stand up to later re-exami-nation.

- The greatest problem is that only satisfaction is enquired about and not the importance of the individual assessment criteria. The assessor therefore does not know how much weight he should place on the individual assessments to be made.

Level 2: Additional questioning about importance
In Level 2, the training participants are asked not only about satisfaction levels, but also about importance.

This method circumvents the problem mentioned in Level 1. The difference between importance and assessment allows conclusions to be made about which criteria suffer from a low satisfaction level or perhaps even reach a satisfaction level beyond their importance. From this one, one can see where too little - or too much - of a good thing exists.

However, empirical investigations have shown that respondents use different yardsticks for importance and for assessment. People assess criteria as "extremely important" far more readily than they assess anything as "excellent". This leads, with the criteria classified as extremely important, to false conclusions. Such criteria are seen as having a greater need of action than is actually the case. A similar situation exists at the lower end of the importance scale.

Level 3: Assessment using the TRI*M GRID
The problem identified under Level 2 is overcome by using the TRI*M GRID. In addition to stated importance, another variable comes into play here. This is "real relevance". It is a measure of the intensity with which an individual assessment criterion influences

overall assessment of a provider using the Index. This "real relevance" is determined using a correlation calculation that draws a link
between the trend in assessments of a criterion and the overall
assessments given by the individual respondents.

In quality assessment of training, three levels can be identified. In
Level 1, the training participants assess various criteria with regard
to their fulfillment by the provider. In Level 2, the participants also
assess the importance of the criteria (using "Stated Importance").
From the difference between importance and assessment, conclusions can be drawn about the urgency of corrective interventions.
Finally, in Level 3, a correlation calculation is used to derive the real
relevance of the criteria from their subjectively biased stated
importance values and to position them - according to stated importance and real relevance - in a coordinate system. From the
arrangement of the criteria in this coordinate system, important conclusions may be drawn, such as "where can savings be made?" and
"where are there Hidden Opportunities?", "which criteria have a
high importance level (Motivators)?", and "which are only seeming-
ly important (Hygienic)?"

Interpretation and graphical representation of survey results using the TRI*M GRID

The basis for a graphical representation of the survey results is the
closed coordinate system in Level 3. The ordinate axis shows stated
importance, while the abscissa carries the scale of real relevance. In
order to position an assessment criterion in this representation, the
arithmetic average value of the individual assessments expressed by
all the respondents is entered on the ordinate as the measure of
stated importance, while on the abscissa the value for real relevance
determined for this criterion from the correlation calculation is
selected.

If this closed coordinate system is subdivided as shown in Level 3,
the assessment criteria distributed over the area correspond to the
four evaluation criteria Potential Savers/?, Hygienics, Motivators
and Hidden Opportunities.

Potential Savers/?
The verbally expressed importance of the assessment criteria falling within this field is low, as is their real significance.

From the low stated importance can be derived the fact that the training participants place low value on the assessment criteria from the outset. Added to this is the fact that these criteria have only a slight influence on the overall result - i.e. their real relevance is also slight. This field can therefore be labeled "Potential Savers/?". In the case of assessment criteria that fall within this field, it is sufficient if the degree of satisfaction is moderate. Being very good in this field means that one has done too much. The field also contains criteria that one considers to be success factors but for which it has not yet been possible to make the customer aware of their importance.

Performance assessment for the individual criteria
It is not sufficient merely to know which assessment criterion falls within which of the observation fields. It is also necessary to bring into this the representation of the third dimension of performance assessment. This is used to make a judgment about how the training participants assess the performance of the trainers according to the individual criteria.

The assessment criterion C (C stands for the Training Center, 1 for the size and furnishings of the training rooms) was evaluated when the training center was built according to the latest state of knowledge as a Motivator. Surprisingly, given the thorough method described here, this criterion fell within the Possible Savings field. Clearly, the expectations of the participants in terms of the size and furnishing of the training rooms had been overestimated. With the benefit of today's viewpoint, savings could have been made when the training center was built. There is, in any event, no need to invest further at present.

A typical hygienic factor is D1 (D: course quality 1: limited number of participants per exercise device). This criterion is assessed with a high verbal relevance. The participants would ideally like to have a device to themselves. In practice, however, it becomes clear that two to three participants per exercise device is regarded as entirely sufficient and even as better, for reasons such as team work and the resulting mutual support.

The assessment criterion D2 (D: course quality 2: balanced proportion of practical exercises) is a Motivator according to the method described here. This underlines the significance of this assessment criterion, which has long been subjectively recognized.

Chart no. 1

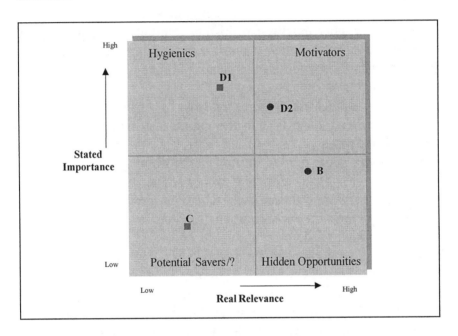

As a third dimension, in the representation one can also introduce assessment of the service given by the training provider. Shown here, with a symbol for each performance assessment criterion, is a sample allocation of the four-assessment criteria equipment of the training center (C), personal attention from the teachers (B), balanced proportion of practical exercises (D2), and number of participants per exercise device (D1).

For this reason, in designing the course in the field of automation technology, the guideline is used that 50% of the time is provided for practical exercises. When the performance assessment is graded as an average value, the difficulty arises of meeting the participants' obviously higher expectations in this regard without making the course unacceptably long.

Surprisingly, the assessment criterion B (B: teachers: personal contact and attention) turned out to be a hidden opportunity. The consequence of this is that the teachers are psychologically trained for this job and today undertake this function more conscientiously and with more focus, even after completion of the course. This means that a teacher must regard his/her training course participant as a pupil who he/she must support with specialist assistance and advice about further specific training possibilities.

In this way, as described here by way of example, all the 25 assessment criteria addressed in the quality assessment system are positioned and assessed. This would, however, have little point if the assessment were only carried out for all the training activities in the training center. After all, one would have no possibility of specifically accessing those sites where corrections are actually needed. Therefore in the questionnaire, nine specialist areas are carefully distinguished: programmable control systems; numerical control; drive technologies; industrial computers; data processing fundamentals; process control systems; measuring, testing and process technologies; data communication; and operation and observation. For each of these specialist areas there is a graphical representation of this type, so that the person responsible for the particular area is able to carry out targeted improvements. And in order that the results of each specialist area can be compared with the overall level, a representation is drawn up in which the overall results of all specialist areas are shown according to the method described.

The introduction of an informative quality assessment system with the help of NFO Infratest

The Automation Technology department at Siemens AG has been making efforts for years to achieve a high quality in training in order, to a large extent, to ensure learning success among course participants and thus to stand out clearly from the mass of service providers in this segment of the training market. Originally, for many years the questionnaire method of assessment described above (Level 1) was practiced, although due to the stated disadvantages, this was never really satisfactory. As a consequence, a specialist external partner was sought for the development and introduction of a powerful quality assessment system.

After long research, the choice was made in favor of NFO Infratest, now known as NFO Infratest. This company had developed the TRI*M method with which it is possible to make qualitative statements about the effects of companies in their markets with regard to customer satisfaction, employee focus and corporate image. NFO Infratest offered good conditions for building up a quality assessment system by modification of this process for gathering and assessing qualitative statements.

The resulting quality assessment system has been practiced for many years and is characterized by the following features:

The assessment takes place in an annual cycle with the following functions: Measuring - Managing - Monitoring. The results are not dependent on accidental or sporadic influences. In a similar way to a control loop using a sampling algorithm, the assessment process brings about - biannually - an iterative movement of the assessment criteria towards an optimal positioning in the coordinate system. As target groups for determining customer orientation, about 2000 to 3000 course participants are questioned every half year; for employee orientation, about 2/3 of the teachers are questioned, and for measuring the corporate image, about 100 of the decision-makers who send participants to such training activities are asked. In the last two of these groups, in each cycle 1/3 of the respondents are left out and, in their place, a corresponding number of new persons from the

150

relevant target group included, so that after every three cycles - among the decision-makers - a completely new respondent group is obtained. This avoids establishing ingrained opinions.

NFO Infratest has alleviated the Automation Technology department of Siemens AG of carrying out this quality assessment work. Fig. 3 shows the process of this cooperation.

Chart no. 2

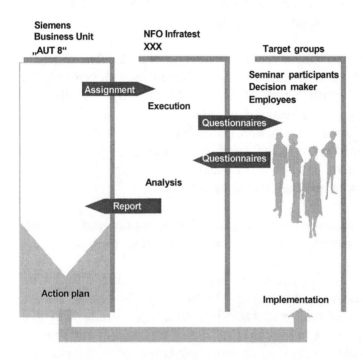

Sequence of the cooperation between Siemens Automation and NFO Infratest for quality assessment in training. NFO Infratest largely takes care of the execution and assessment of quality assessment itself and, based on the results, suggests quality-improving measures that Siemens then puts into practice.

Following contract award, the drawing up of the questionnaire for the three target groups - course participants, decision-makers, company staff - was the most difficult and important task. The questions had to be carefully formulated so that the answers would be unambiguous.

The cyclical quality assessment system based on this questionnaire is mainly carried out by NFO Infratest itself. Only the issuing of questionnaire forms to participants in the courses selected by NFO is done by the relevant Siemens training staff. Everything else is done by NFO Infratest, thus also ensuring the neutrality of the questions. Every year, NFO Infratest draws up a report for the management of the training center and simultaneously makes suggestions for quality-enhancing measures.

In the Automation Technology division at Siemens AG, this process has the following advantages:

- As far as is known, this is the first time that this process has been used to assess and control training services on a broad base and in a thorough and systematical manner.

- NFO Infratest is a neutral partner. No one among the leaders at Siemens affected by the results can feel themselves to be disadvantaged in any way.

- For Siemens it is better and cheaper to buy in this service from a specialist supplier than to do the job itself with the extra statisticians this would require.

The process proved itself so useful, after a short introductory period, that since 1993 it has been applied not only in the central training centers at Nürnberg-Moorenbrunn and Karlsruhe, but in all training centers for the Automation Technology division in Germany. Its spread across the world is now so advanced that the leading countries in the field of automation, such as France, the Netherlands, Great Britain and the USA are also linked into the same systematic process.

Druck: Strauss Offsetdruck, Mörlenbach
Verarbeitung: Schäffer, Grünstadt